95

WANTED

Sally Clark

Talonbooks
2004

Talonbooks
P.O. Box 2076, Vancouver, British Columbia, Canada V6B 3S3
www.talonbooks.com

Typeset in New Baskerville and printed and bound in Canada.
Printed on 100% post-consumer recycled paper.

First Printing: August 2004

Library and Archives of Canada Cataloguing in Publication
Clark, Sally, 1953–
        Wanted / Sally Clark.

A play.
ISBN 0-88922-503-6

        I. Title.
PS8555.L37197W35 2004   C812'.54   C2004-903256-9

The publisher gratefully acknowledges the financial support of the
Canada Council for the Arts; the Government of Canada through the
Book Publishing Industry Development Program; and the Province of
British Columbia through the British Columbia Arts Council for our
publishing activities.

Acknowledgements

I would like to thank Pierre Berton, Steve Robertson and the members of the Berton House Committee for generously allowing me to stay in the Berton House Writer's Retreat in Dawson City during the Winter and Spring of 2002.

Many thanks also to the Canada Council for awarding me the Residency Grant at Nakai Theatre.

I would like to thank Chapelle Jaffe and Karl Siegler for their expertise and encouragement.

Thanks also to: David Curtis, KIAC, Paula Hazard, Martin Kinch, Brian Richmond, Scott Malcolm, The Dawson City Museum, Nakai Theatre and the Playwrights Theatre Centre in Vancouver (where two readings were held on June 26, 2002 and September 26, 2002), and to the actors for the readings in Whitehorse and Vancouver.

Finally, I would like to thank Michael Clark who brought me back to the Yukon and urged me to write this play. I treasure his support and encouragement.

Foreword

Departures and Whirlpools

Sally Clark's plays are known for large casts, numerous scenes, twisted endings and unsettling dark humour amid tragic circumstances. Her heroines are thrust into mad worlds where the law, the media, organized religion, science and medicine—those touchstones upon which we have placed our twenty-first century "faiths"—mysteriously, systematically and murderously conspire. There is no way out, no way to succeed, because to live outside of dystopia is to live nowhere, to live not at all. The paradox is that while complete freedom is impossible in an organized society, the organized society in Clark's plays creates a sense of swirling chaos.

Wanted, however, marks a departure from Clark's previous work. Though the characters and the scenes remain numerous, and the chaos no less threatening, the story follows both a heroine, Mary Potter, and two brothers, Jack and Joe, whose lives are as important to the play as Mary's. The focus seems less to do with systemic chaos than with cooperation and relationships. Though chaos is found in the whirlpool image that opens the play, the momentum is inward, introspective—but no less frantic.

Wanted could be considered Clark's first "Canadian" play. Set during the Klondike Gold Rush of 1897, the play uncovers part of our country's history while capturing the thrills and the anguish that characterized the period. Family and friends came together and were wrenched apart for the promise of great wealth. Many died poor and hungry for their efforts.

But while Clark restages part of Canada's history in *Wanted*, the language is decidedly contemporary: "completely true to its Gold Rush setting, yet totally modern in its sensibilities," wrote Pierre Berton concerning an early draft of the play. We recognize ourselves, especially our innocence and our determination, in these characters precisely because we see ourselves in their speech patterns, their interactions and in—dare I say—a *Canadian* humour— amid challenging circumstances. These characters are parts of us. The play uses its Klondike regionalism to strike national, even universal chords on themes of difference, compassion and mutual survival: where we are from determines who we are, but where we are going—if we will go anywhere— depends on each other.

When *Wanted* opened in March 2003 in Whitehorse (later playing in its historic setting of Dawson City at the 105-year-old Palace Grand Theatre) it marked two milestones in the career of one of Canada's most recognizable playwrights. The first is that *Wanted* is Clark's tenth professionally produced play; the second is that it marked the twentieth year of Clark's playwriting career—a remarkable career that has, thus far, spanned from Toronto to Vancouver to Whitehorse. To date, her body of work has treated remarkably diverse topics—ranging from the larger-than-life personalities Joan of Arc, Artemisia Gentileschi and Frances Farmer to the Kafka-inspired Judith K.; to purely original characters named Hannah ("Zombie"), Val and Moo—with a remarkably consistent dark comic voice. Sally Clark's imaginative worlds are as chaotic as whirlpools, and they do pull you in.

Robin Whittaker
Toronto, August 2004

Wanted was first produced by Nakai Theatre, in Whitehorse Yukon Territories from March 26 to April 5, 2003. It played in Whitehorse from March 26 to March 30, then went on tour through the Yukon, ending with a performance at the Palace Grand in Dawson City with the following cast and crew:

MARY POTTER	Vanessa Holmes*
JACK MALONE	Brian Fidler
JOE MCALISTER	Tom Scholte*
WOMAN 1	Amanda Leslie
MAN 1	James McCullough
MAN 2	Keith Wyatt

Directed by Michael Clark
Set, Lights & Props Designer: David Skelton
Costume Designer: Alma Newton
Sound Designer: Daniel Janke
Production Manager: Moira Sauer
Stage Manager: Dean Eyre

* Ms. Holmes and Mr. Scholte appeared courtesy of Canadian Actor's Equity Association.

Playwright's Notes

Michael Clark called me in Toronto in the fall of 2000 to ask if I would be interested in writing a play about the Klondike. I had just returned from a stay in Berton House in Dawson City. I had fallen in love with the North and was very inspired by it. Michael suggested that I apply to be playwright-in-residence at Nakai.

Steve Robertson and the Berton House Committee graciously allowed me to stay in Berton House the winter of 2001/02. The house has an extensive library on Klondike material, from which I drew the inspiration for this play. Pierre Berton's robust and exciting history of the Klondike gave me a real sense of the period. His book brought the Klondike characters to life. I was fascinated by the tales of the losers, the people who joined The Great Stampede, tried to find gold, then gave up and went home. I wrote my play *Wanted* during that winter.

A Brief History

That first winter of the Stampede was particularly bad. The gold was actually discovered in August of 1896, but it took until July 17, 1897 for the news to reach the Outside. Within ten days, the city ports were crammed with thousands of people, clamouring to get on ships headed for the Klondike, so they could get to Dawson City before the Yukon River froze. The Stampeders did not know that all the claims were staked.They brought just enough food for the journey, thinking they could buy food and supplies when they arrived. However, that year, the supply boats got stranded on sand dunes and people robbed the boats.

After a long, perilous journey, a 'cheechako' would arrive in Dawson and discover that there was no gold, no food and no work.

Characters

MARY POTTER, *a young woman, 18 years old*
JACK MALONE, *a young man in his early twenties*
JOE MCALLISTER, *Jack's half-brother, early thirties*

Act One: MAN 1, WOMAN 1, WOMAN 2, MAN IN SCOW, HANK HALLIDAY, PETE SMITH, LOUSETOWN MAN 1, LOUSETOWN MAN 2.

Act Two: DAWSON SALOON MAN, EXECUTIONER, HANGED MAN, DIAMOND TOOTH GERTIE, BARKEEPER (Jake), PROSPECTOR 1 (Roy), PROSPECTOR 2 (Bert), ANOTHER MAN, PASSING MAN (goldfields), EDDY (offstage voice), BARTENDER PETE (of Pete's Place), RELUCTANT DANCING MEN, SWIFTWATER BILL, FRED, GERTIE'S GIRLS, GRAVEYARD BOSS, DOCTOR, CHAMPAGNE MAN.

Nakai Theatre staged this play with six actors; the assorted parts were performed with a CHORUS of two men and two women.

Setting

Time: late Summer 1897 to Winter 1898
Place: Banks of the Yukon River and Dawson City.
Act One: Miles Canyon, Lake Labarge, Five Finger Rapids, one day out of Dawson City and Lousetown.
Act Two: Dawson City and Klondike Goldfields.

Running Time

The running time of *Wanted* is 60–65 minutes for Act One and 50 minutes for Act Two.

ACT ONE

Scene 1

Past. 1897. CHORUS. Lights up on MAN 1.

MAN 1:

(*announces*) WANTED: a young lady or widow, not over thirty, unencumbered and matrimonially inclined to accompany an able-bodied forty-year-old prospector to the Klondike.

Lights up on WOMAN 1.

WOMAN 1:

Yes. I am willing to get married and go to the Klondike. I have read everything in the papers about the gold up there and I am free to confess. I want some of it.

CHORUS:

WANTED.

Lights up on WOMAN 2.

WOMAN 2:

I look at the matter this way. By getting right down to hard work, we could, in a year or two, accumulate enough to live in comfort the rest of our days.

While she speaks, TWO MEN come in and look WOMAN 2 over.

WOMAN 2:

> We are both young enough to see a good deal of
> happiness and yet old enough to have gotten over
> romancing. Yes, if you come up to my expectations—
> and, by the way, I don't look for perfection in any
> man: we all have our faults.

> *The MEN decide she is not worth the effort and leave.*

WOMAN 2:

> I am willing to chance it—you, marriage, the Klondike
> and all. *(looks up, is disappointed when she sees the men
> have gone away)*

CHORUS:

> WANTED.

> *Lights up on MARY POTTER.*

MARY:

> My name is Mary Potter. I am eighteen years old,
> sturdy but comely. I am used to hardship. I am very
> unencumbered. My family are all dead. I think I could
> be a helpmate to you and the union would be of
> advantage to me, for I find it a hard struggle in this
> world, without relatives, though my friends are kind, it
> is not like having some one all your own.

Scene 2

> *A scow travelling on the Yukon River, at the entrance to
> Miles Canyon and the White Horse Rapids. MARY is
> with two other women and two men in the scow. MAN 1
> stands in the front. He paddles and steers the scow. A
> MAN is at the back of the scow with two women. MARY
> is in the centre.*

MARY:

It's so peaceful.

MAN 1:

Till you started yakkin'. Supposed to be a canyon up ahead. Supposed to be marked.

WOMAN 1:

Oh my! We're moving swiftly.

MARY:

(*points to a sign*) Is that the sign?

MAN 1:

(*turns to look*) Where? (*suddenly looks ahead*)

There is a sudden, crashing sound of water falling from a great height.

MAN 1:

(*sees a sudden drop and a whirling mass of rapids*) Oh CHRIST!

The WOMEN clutch onto the sides of the scow and scream.

MAN 1:

(*paddling furiously in an attempt to steer*) Cut yer caterwauling and hold tight! (*to the MAN at the back*) Hey, Girly Man! Get yer oar in gear!

The MAN IN BACK tries to paddle. Everyone lurches forward, then lurches back; veer to one side, then the other. WOMAN 1 and 2 shriek. MAN 1 in front struggles to maintain control of the scow.

MAN 1:

(*shouting*) S'okay! We're gonna be all right! (*paddling faster*) I just need to keep us clear of this here whirlpo-o-o-OOOAAAAAAAAHHHH!!!

There is a deafening sound of water crashing and churning.

NOTE: The special effect one wants to create is five people in a scow being spun around by a whirlpool. Everyone falls out of the scow except for MARY. The scow flies through the air and crashes in the river below—breaking into pieces.

Everyone except for MARY screams and raises their arms.

DETAILS: When the scow first hits the whirlpool, it moves in a circle and picks up speed as it spins. THE WOMEN (except for MARY) scream. WOMAN 1 falls into the whirlpool. The MAN AT THE BACK of the scow (referred to as GIRLY MAN) falls in. The boat spins at a dizzying speed and is finally flung out of the whirlpool, into the depths below. The remaining WOMEN and MAN 1 (FRANK STANDISH) scream and try to cling onto the scow. It crash-lands and breaks up into pieces. FRANK and the WOMEN disappear into the water and drown except for MARY who miraculously survives.

Blackout.

Scene 3

September, 1897. The banks of the Yukon River, below Miles Canyon.

Inside a small tent. There are two areas of stacked-up spruce boughs which act as beds. A Yukon stove is in the middle of the tent. A rough-looking man in his early thirties (JOE MCALLISTER) tends it.

Lights up on JACK MALONE, a man in his mid twenties.
He holds a dripping wet MARY in his arms. He gazes
down at her, as if he has fished a prize out of the river.

JACK:

(*to MARY*) It was a miracle you made it.

JOE:

(*spins around*) What the hell—

JACK:

(*puts MARY down*) Best you get out of those clothes
and stand by the stove.

MARY looks at JOE.

JOE:

What's she doing here!

JACK:

(*turns JOE around*) Turn around, Joe. No peeking. The
lady's shy.

He throws MARY some clothes. She stares at them in
stupefaction.

JACK:

Quick! You must change. (*turns his back on her, turns*
JOE around again) It's dangerous to be in wet clothes
up here.

MARY undresses and hurriedly puts on JACK's clothes.

MARY:

Why is it dangerous?

JOE:

It's not dangerous.

JACK:

One of the old timers told me. You're not supposed to
get wet. Not even sweat. 'Cause the sweat freezes and
kills you.

MARY:

Oh.

JOE:

When it's 40 below. When it's fucking cold out—

JACK:

Joe!

JOE:

When it's cold outside, then, it's dangerous.

JACK:

It's pretty cold. And I bet that water was cold—

JOE:

What the hell's going on? What's she doing here!

JACK:

Oh, that's quite a story, Joe. She's one lucky lady.

MARY:

(*to JACK*) You saved my life, Mr. Malone!

JOE:

Did he, now?

JACK:

You shoulda seen it, Joe. It was awful. I heard all this commotion. People were screaming—"Squaw's got another one" so I had to go look see.

JOE:

You had to go look, eh.

JACK:

Well yeah.

JOE:

Always looking. Always stopping to have a look-see. And what good's it do ya? Just hangs us back. You had to get mad at that guy and his horse.

JACK:

He was flogging her.

JOE:

Yeah. So. Had to get her to move.

JACK:

She was dying. He was flaying her alive.

JOE:

So, it's not your lookout. What claim that horse have on you, eh? Nuthin'. You're a tender-hearted fool. It's your mother what done that to ya. Brought you up soft.

JACK:

She brought you up, too.

JOE:

Yeah, well, she was tough on me. Didn't like me. And now, you bring in another set of problems. 'Nother goddamn mare.

JACK:

How'd you know her name was Mary?

JOE:

Huh?

JACK:

Mary Potter, this here's my brother, Joe McAllister.

MARY:

(*to JACK*) Isn't your name Malone?

JACK:

(*hurriedly*) Yes. Anyways ...

JOE:

(*tersely*) We're half-brothers. Are you dressed yet?

MARY:

Yes.

MARY shivers as she draws near the stove. She places her shoes and socks near the stove.

JOE:

Good. (*goes to her and pushes her towards the tent flap*) Now, get out!

JACK:

Joe?! What are you doing?!

JOE:

Sending her back out where she came from.

JACK:

Joe! She doesn't have any shoes on.

JOE grabs MARY's shoes and socks and shoves them at her.

JACK:

But Joe, she's still shivering. (*whispers to JOE*) I said she could stay the night.

JOE:

Well, I say she can't! One night leads to the next and before long, we've got a woman in tow. And a woman'll always slow you down. 'Sides, we don't have enough grub to feed three.

MARY:

I won't stay long.

JOE:

Hey! I'm talking to my brother. Not you. (*to JACK*) You were supposed to get wood.

JACK:

It's outside.

JOE:

Bring it in.

JACK leaves for a moment. MARY looks apprehensively at JOE who glares at her. JACK brings the wood in and speaks while he's doing this.

JACK:

Joe, you shoulda been there. This scow went into The Squaw and there're all these people on it, screaming their heads off and The Squaw's just toying with them. Spinning them round and round. Some of them lost their balance and The Squaw just sucked them in.

MARY starts to cry.

JACK:

Sorry, Miss, but I gotta make Joe understand. People were laying bets. She had some Swedes for four hours before she spat them out. You guys must have been spinning for fifteen, twenty minutes 'fore I got there. Anyways—and you can correct me here, Miss, if I'm wrong but your scow suddenly flew out of her, borne on the air, like it was gushing out of a geyser.

MARY:

Really?

JACK:

Oh yeah, it floated on the air, for just a moment. Then smack! It hit the river and more people fell in. Except for you, Miss. You clung on. It was a sight. That beaten-up old scow ricocheting from one boulder to another, losing big chunks of herself each time. And still, you hung on. You got tenacity, Miss! When we could finally get at you, some of the lads got a rope—

MARY:

You got the rope.

JACK:

Well, yeah. I guess I did. The others helped.

MARY:

No. You did it. I saw you.

JACK:

Anyways—you caught it and held on. It was a miracle!

MARY:

I was so frightened. I could never have done it without you. Your gentle voice. Coaxing me in to shore. You saved my life.

JACK:

Aw, now—

MARY:

You did. Those other folk wouldn't have done anything. You were so brave!

JACK:

You were like a mermaid, the way you—

JOE:

'Scuse me while I vomit.

JACK:

Joe! (*to MARY*) He's got a peculiar sense of humour.

MARY:

I should probably go.

JACK:

No, please! Don't go. (*to JOE*) Come on, Joe. That's one terrible ordeal she's been through. So, she's gotta settle down for a spell. One night. Okay?

JOE:

(*sighs*) You ask for trouble and you gets it.

JACK:

Thanks, Joe!

> *MARY looks confused. JACK motions that it's okay for her to stay.*

JACK:

    I'll get your bedding.

MARY:

    But it's all gone.

JACK:

    You'll see. (*goes to leave*) I'll make you a bed.

MARY:

    (*grabs her shoes and starts to put them on*) I'll come with you!

JACK:

    You stay by the stove. You're still shivering.

JOE:

    Maybe, she don't want a bed. Maybe, she wants to sleep with you, Jacky boy. (*chuckles nastily*)

JACK:

    None of that talk, see! She's a lady. (*leaves*)

JOE:

    (*grumbles*) Yeah, right. A lady. (*looks MARY up and down*) So, what can you do?

MARY:

    Do?

JOE:

    Yeah, you gotta earn your keep. Even if it is for the one night. Got anything special you do at night? (*approaches*)

MARY:

    I can cook.

JOE:

    That so? Well, see what you can make of that. (*points to the food supply*)

MARY rummages through the food bags. JACK enters with an armful of spruce boughs and arranges them into a bed.

MARY:

You're making a bed?

JACK:

Yeah. If you fix them up right, they're nice and soft. Like a mattress.

MARY:

Oh, you're so clever.

JACK:

It's nothing.

JOE:

I showed him how to do it.

MARY:

You did?

JOE:

Yeah. So now, Mary, how 'bout you cook us some supper.

MARY:

Mrs. Standish is my name. I would appreciate you calling me by that. Shows respect.

JOE:

Ooooo Respect! We gotta respect you now, OoooooWeeee. Trouble—this is trouble, Jack.

JACK:

(*to MARY*) I thought you said your name was Potter.

MARY:

Yes. It was. Force of habit. I haven't been married long.

JOE:

Out of sight, out of mind, eh? Your husband croaks in The Squaw and it's Miss Potter. 'Cept when you want RESPECT—Ooooo, then suddenly you're married. One of those marriages of convenience?

MARY bursts into tears.

JOE:

We'll never get our dinner at this rate.

JOE gets up and pushes MARY aside.

JOE:

Blubber somewheres else. You're getting the cornmeal wet. (*Starts making dinner*)

JACK:

Ah—Mrs. Standish. You can lie down on my bed for a while.

JACK gently places MARY on his bed and puts a blanket over her.

MARY:

I'll leave in the morning.

JACK:

Don't mind, Joe. You get some sleep. (*walks over to JOE*) (*under his breath*) Jesus Joe, why do you have to be so mean alla time?

JOE:

I ain't mean. I'm careful.

Short passage of time—can be indicated by light fade.

Later. MARY is fast asleep. JOE makes the dinner.

JOE:

I got a bad feeling 'bout that girl.

JACK:

You get bad feelings about everyone.

JOE:

Her surviving something like that—everyone else is killed and she survives ...

JACK:

It's luck.

JOE:

Yeah, luck.

> *JOE fusses with his cooking, then suddenly stops as if he's solved a riddle.*

JOE:

She's a Hoodoo!

JACK:

Whowhat?

JOE:

A Hoodoo. That's what she is all right. It's been nagging at me and I couldn't put a name to it. Hoodoo. Yeah. Hoodoo. That's what she is.

JACK:

So?

JOE:

So, don't you think it's mighty queer. Her coming clear of something like that. The folks she's with is all dead and she floats in to shore.

JACK:

Well, it wasn't quite that way. I had to haul in and get her.

JOE:

So, you say she's lucky, right?

JACK:

    Yeah.

JOE:

    Well, let's just turn it around for a second. Them
    other folks were unlucky, right?

JACK:

    Yeah.

JOE:

    Mighty unlucky.

JACK:

    Yeah.

JOE:

    Well, something give them folks all that bad luck. And
    that Something is right over there. (*points to MARY,
    whispers*) That's a Hoodoo.

JACK:

    (*looks at MARY*) Naw, she ain't no Hoodoo.

JOE:

    Squaw took her in and spat her out. She's a Hoodoo.

JACK:

    You're talking crazy, Joe.

JOE:

    I'm telling ya. She marries this fellah and a couple
    days later—

JACK:

    We don't know how long she was married.

JOE:

    Long enough to forget it ever happened. Not long.
    And he and all his kith 'n kin wind up dead.

JACK:

    We don't know if those other people were his family.

JOE:

What sort of woman marries a guy on the Trail?

JACK:

We don't know they married on the Trail.

JOE:

She was Miss—not that long ago. Probably came up here to get married and what kinda woman would do that.

JACK:

I don't know.

JOE:

A woman with no family. And what happened to them, I wonder?

JACK:

Jesus Joe, you're making my head spin. Is supper ready yet?

JOE:

Yeah. I guess so.

JACK:

(*looks inside pot, is disappointed*) Oh. Beans.

JOE:

Yeah, beans. Who's cooking this meal?

JACK:

You are, Joe.

JOE:

Better wake up the Hoodoo.

JACK:

Don't call her that! (*goes over to her*) Poor thing. She's just conked out. (*goes closer, puts hand on her forehead*) She's feverish. Do you think she'll be all right?

JOE:

>Oh—She'll be fine. It's us you should be worried about.

JACK:

>(*softly*) Mrs. Standish?

MARY:

>Mmmmm (*moans*)

JACK:

>Just sit up for a little bit. (*goes to the stove, dishes out some beans on a plate and brings it to her*) Here's some beans.

MARY:

>Thank you. (*takes a mouthful*) Oh! (*clutches her mouth and laughs*)

JACK:

>What is it?

MARY:

>Oh, it's nothing. I think I might have broken my tooth.

JOE:

>And you're laughing about it?

JACK:

>That's awful. (*loudly to JOE*) That's a very unlucky thing to have happen to you.

JOE:

>She's laughing.

MARY:

>It's all right. I didn't. I was surprised, is all—I-ah— (*starts to laugh*) haven't had beans like that since— (*laughs hysterically*)

JACK:

>Since when?

MARY:

Since my father died. (*laughs and cries simultaneously*)

JOE:

Oh yeah, we've got a live one here. Helluva funny story 'bout your dad dying.

JACK:

She's hysterical, Joe. Calm down, Miss—I mean—Mrs. Standish—calm down—it's gonna be all right.

MARY is still laughing and crying.

JACK:

Bring us a cup of tea, Joe. That might settle her down.

JOE grudgingly hands a tin mug to JACK. JACK places the mug in front of MARY.

JACK:

Here's some tea. Would you like that?

MARY calms down enough to look at the cup of tea. She takes it gingerly and stares at it.

JACK:

It won't hurt ya. Honest. (*to JOE*) You didn't make it too hot, did you, Joe?

JOE:

It's tea. It's supposed to be hot.

MARY:

(*takes a sip*) Thank you. I'm sorry. I wasn't expecting the beans to be like that.

JACK:

Like what? Rock hard?

MARY:

(*smiles*) You're supposed to soak them.

JOE:

I soak 'em. I put 'em in a pan of water while I'm heating up the stove. And then I boil the living Jesus out of them.

JACK:

Watch your language, Joe.

MARY:

You're supposed to soak them overnight.

JOE:

Overnight?!

MARY:

Yes. Even for a day or two, if you want.

JACK:

That long? Say, are you really a cook?

MARY:

I know about beans and I guess I could look at what you've got and put something together. I used to watch our cook when I was little. I was fascinated by him—how he—

JOE:

Your family had a cook?

MARY:

Till my father died. Then, mother had to learn and well ... she experimented.

JOE:

Pretty hoity toity, were you?

MARY:

Just hoity. Not toity.

JACK:

(*bursts out laughing*) Got you there, Joe.

JOE:

Yeah—funny cuts, aren't ya? So, who else was on that scow with you?

MARY looks at JOE, does not answer.

JACK:

Joe!

JOE:

Your husband, for one. His family? Your family?

MARY puts the cup of tea down.

MARY:

I'm feeling a bit dizzy. Thank you for the shelter. I'm sure that, in the morning, the people on the Trail will be happy to answer your questions and add their own personal conjectures to the situation. And now, if you will excuse me, please, I'm going to sleep. (*turns her face to the tent wall—away from JACK and JOE*)

JOE:

Her Majesty speaks.

JACK:

Let's turn in, Joe.

JACK lies down on a spruce bough bed. JOE stares at MARY who sleeps.

Scene 4

Inside the tent. The next morning. MARY has her own clothes on. She stands near the stove area. She is preparing breakfast. JACK's bed is very near the stove. He wakes up, as he hears MARY move about.

JACK:

Whatcha doing?

MARY:

Ssh. Don't want to wake up your brother. Not till they're done.

JACK gets up. (He has worn his clothes to bed) He stands beside MARY and helps her with breakfast. They speak quietly.

MARY:

You've been very kind to me. I can't thank you enough.

JACK:

You're not leaving?

MARY:

Um—it's awkward—your brother seems to dislike me.

JACK:

That's nothing special. He hates everyone.

MARY:

Why?

JACK:

I don't know. He's always been that way.

MARY:

Must have been hard to live with.

JACK:

Didn't see much of him. He left home when I was little.

MARY:

You're seeing a lot of him, now.

JACK:

Ain't that the truth. You can't make a trip like this by yourself, though. I woulda been a goner for sure, if it hadn't been for Joe. (*slight pause*) If it's just Joe you're worried about, he's at his worst when he first meets people. His bark is worse than his bite.

MARY:

It is. Until you get bitten.

JACK:

(*laughs*) Oops! Gotta be quiet. Don't want to wake up the dog.

MARY and JACK giggle together.

JACK:

I haven't laughed since I got here. You got a lot of fun in you, Mary Potter. Stay for me. Please.

MARY:

I don't know. (*puts pancakes on a plate*) Here. Give these to your brother. Put what he likes on them first.

JACK:

(*walks over to JOE*) Sit up, Joe. Got a present for you.

JOE:

(*groggy*) Mmmph.

JACK:

Joe.

JOE sits up. (JOE also is fully dressed) JACK gives him the plate. JOE looks down at the plate suspiciously, tries a mouthful, then starts to eat voraciously.

MARY:

Don't forget the coffee. (*holds out a cup*)

JACK goes over to MARY, takes the cup and gives it to JOE who hands back the empty plate.

JACK:

Guess you like them, eh, Joe?

JOE:

Needs more syrup.

JACK:

Well, that was my fault. I put the fixings on.

*JACK walks back to MARY who replenishes JOE's plate.
JACK puts syrup on, brings it back to JOE—who is now
drinking his coffee and staring thoughtfully at MARY.
JOE takes the plate from JACK and eats slowly this time,
savouring each mouthful, still not taking his eyes off
MARY.*

*JACK goes to MARY. She hands him a plate of pancakes.
He sits on his makeshift bed and starts to eat.*

*MARY goes to her bed (JACK's old bed) and eats her
portion.*

JACK:

(*after a mouthful*) My God! (*takes another*) My God!
These are the best blazin' pancakes I ever had. What'd
you put in 'em? They got bounce.

MARY:

Baking soda.

JACK:

Really? We tried a whole lot of that stuff. Made them
taste awful. All foamy and nasty.

MARY:

(*grins*) You're only supposed to use a little.

JACK:

Oooh. Well, that explains it. (*takes another bite*) Aren't
they good, Joe? Aren't they the best pancakes you ever
had?

JOE:

(*costs him to say this*) Yeah. They're not bad.

JACK:

(*takes a sip of coffee*) Coffee! This is coffee!

JOE:

Aw Cripes, Jack! It's not the Holy Eucharist! Stop
carrying on! You sound like an idiot! Yes, it's coffee.
Mrs. Standish makes a nice pot of coffee. (*sips his coffee
and looks at MARY intently*) How's your carrying? Are
you strong?

MARY:

I can carry. 'Course, I lost my pack ...

JOE:

We can rig something up for you. (*pause*) Ah—(*clears
throat*) Mrs. Standish?

MARY:

Yes?

JOE:

Um—would you like to join us for a spell?

MARY:

Well ... for a time. Yes. Thank you, Mr. McAllister.

JOE:

(*nods*) Good. Good. (*gets up nervously, to JACK*) We was
gonna shoot the Rapids but think we'll portage
around them, instead. Got an extra hand, so it won't
take as long.

MARY:

Excuse me, please. (*hums a tune to herself as she leaves
the tent*)

> JOE and JACK are momentarily puzzled, then realize that
> MARY has gone out to relieve herself.

JACK:

So, you don't think she's bad luck, now, do you, Joe?

JOE:

> I ain't sure what I think. She made a damn fine breakfast and if supper's as good, then she's worth having around for a while.

> *Pause.*

JOE:

> But don't you go getting sweet on her. I see you looking at her.

JACK:

> Why not? Why can't I get sweet on her, if I like. I'm free. She's free.

JOE:

> Yeah. Free 'n easy. She ain't got a cent to her name.

JACK:

> You don't know. That fellah, Standish, might have left her some money.

JOE:

> You think Standish was rich, eh?

JACK:

> Could be.

JOE:

> Packing through the Chilkoot? Dream on! Now, Jack, The smart thing to do is to concentrate on why you're here. You get the gold first. Then, you look for a woman. And when we get that big pan-out, we can take a steamer down to 'Frisco and get our women there. Better selection—

> *MARY enters. The men look guilty but she gives no indication that she has heard anything.*

JOE:

> I gotta check the boat.

JOE leaves the tent. JACK and MARY start packing up.

JACK:

I'm glad you're staying. I was wondering how you'd cope on your own.

MARY:

You were worried about me?

JACK:

Of course. Alone ... the men ...

MARY:

Oh, they wouldn't give me any trouble. They've got no eyes for anything but the path ahead. It's like they're possessed. All in a trance, heads down, plodding along. Keep moving, keep moving. I'm not a woman to them. I'm just something that stands in the way of the gold. More like, I'd get trampled to death.

They laugh and pack for a bit.

MARY:

Your brother's like that. He's got the fever. Now he's seen a use for me, I can stay. An extra pair of hands.

JACK:

Ha! That's what he said when he sent for me.

MARY:

Why'd you go?

JACK:

When your big brother invites you on an adventure, you go! And of course, there's the gold. Facing a sure thing of being poor for the rest of my life up against a gamble of being rich—why not take it? What have I got to lose?

MARY:

Your life.

JACK:

Well—yes. I can see that, now. But back with the family in 'Frisco, that didn't seem likely. I went up to Seattle to meet him. Hadn't laid eyes on him since I was seven. He spotted me. I would never have known him. He'd changed so.

MARY:

How?

JACK:

Well, he used to be wild. But I liked that. He was always getting in trouble 'n telling people off. One time, my dad's friend kept at him to get his hair cut. Joe liked the long hair—Wild Bill Hickock style. Always wanted to be an outlaw. Anyways, Dad's friend gives Joe a dollar 'n says, "Here's a dollar. Get yourself a haircut." And fast as you can spit, Joe whips into his pocket 'n pulls out some money 'n says, "Here's two dollars. Never speak to me again."

MARY gasps and laughs.

JACK:

(*laughs*) The look on that guy's face. It was something to behold. I was amazed Joe had two bucks, just sitting in his pocket to give away like that. 'Course he caught hell 'n all. But it was worth it. He's not so rebellious, now. Just seems angry most of the time.

MARY:

Is he a prospector?

JACK:

No—he just drifted around, doing odd jobs. Seems like the whole country quit their jobs overnight to come up here.

MARY:

Yes.

Pause.

JACK:

You're very brave.

MARY:

Pardon?

JACK:

Not many women got the courage to join their husbands.

MARY:

I'm not brave. Foolish, more likely.

JACK:

You said you weren't married long.

MARY:

That's right.

JACK:

Um—how long?

MARY:

I'm sorry—but I can't—it pains me to talk about it, Mr. Malone.

JACK:

Oh. (*pause*) You don't trust me.

MARY:

Of course, I trust you. You're an answer to my prayers, Mr. Malone.

JACK:

Please—when it's just you and me, call me Jack. Please. Our secret.

MARY:

All right.

JACK:

And can I call you Mary?

MARY:

When we're alone. Yes.

JACK:

(*takes MARY's hand and kisses it*) Mary. (*looks at her and smiles*) Mary Potter.

MARY:

Mary Sta—

JACK:

No. (*gently plays with her hand*) Mary Potter. You're a good woman, Mary Potter.

MARY:

No. No, I'm not. (*drops her hand*)

JACK:

Why would you say that?

MARY:

You don't know what I was praying for. (*turns away and resumes packing*)

    JOE enters.

JACK:

How's it look, Joe?

JOE:

We can manage.

    He helps with the packing.

JOE:

Um—ah ... this here situation—it might get a little awkward explaining it to people.

MARY:

Pardon?

JOE:

Well—ah—people might get to wondering why there's a Mr. Malone, a Mr. McAllister and a Mrs. Standish in one tent.

MARY:

It's none of their business, is it?

JOE:

Well, people make things their business and …

MARY:

Your point, Mr. McAllister?

JOE:

I—ah—I—ah think it would draw less attention to ourselves if say, two of us had the same last name. So, I thought—ah—that maybe we should tell people that you were my—ah—

MARY & JOE:

(*together*)   MARY: Cousin?
                        JOE: Wife.

JACK & MARY:

(*together*) YOUR WIFE?!

MARY:

Mr. Standish not dead a day and you want me to deny him?! What sort of woman do you take me for? (*starts to cry*)

JOE:

Oh, God—she's off again.

JACK:

Oh—Ma—Mrs. Standish. Joe didn't mean it that way. (*glares at JOE*) He was trying to—well, I don't know what he was trying to do but he's sorry. Aren't you, Joe?

JOE:

> (*confused*) Yeah—I didn't mean to offend. I just thought it would make—but Cousin! That's a good one. Never thought of you being a cousin. Guess I never had any. Guess that's why …

Scene 5

> *Portage trail around White Horse Rapids. JACK, JOE and MARY haul their stuff. JOE is ahead. JACK and MARY lag behind.*

MARY:

> Isn't it beautiful!

JACK:

> It surely is.

MARY:

> The trees on that mountain are such a bright shade of yellow. It's like ribbons.

JACK:

> Yeah. And each day, there's more of them. That whole side will be bright yellow.
>
> *JOE is quietly getting annoyed.*

MARY:

> I wonder why there's no red.

JACK:

> Funny 'bout that. I've seen red on others. A deep purple-red, comes from this flowering weed that covers—

JOE:

> (*erupts*) AW GEEZ! Shut your gobs, would ya! All this yakking's gonna put us behind.

MARY:

    (*jokingly to JACK*) Can't fall behind. Someone might get there ahead of us. Might put a claim in before we get there. Might get the very last claim in all of the Klondike. And we missed it, 'cause we paused. Stopped to look at the scenery. Hurry, hurry, hurry!

JOE:

    YES! Hurry! The goddamn river's going to freeze up and if we don't get down it while it's running, we'll be stuck in this friggin' wilderness. Stranded. You can look at the scenery all you like, then. You can look at it till you rot.

MARY:

    The river's going to freeze?

JOE:

    That's what the Injuns is saying.

JACK:

    But it's only September. It's warm out.

JOE:

    Yeah. Today. Here. Wasn't warm on the Chilkoot.

MARY:

    It still seems odd.

JOE:

    It freezes from below, see.

MARY:

    It what?

JOE:

    From the bottom. The river bottom's already frozen and it's just waiting for the air above to get just a little cold. Then you get the cold coming on both sides. River freezes in its tracks. You don't want to be on it when that happens.

MARY:

Oh.

JOE:

So, there's a reason for hurrying.

MARY:

Oh.

JOE:

I don't look around. I ask around. Learn more by asking than by looking.

MARY does not respond. They travel in silence for a bit.

JOE:

(*to MARY*) How many people were in your party?

MARY does not answer.

JACK:

Mrs. Standish? How many people were in your scow?

MARY:

Um—five.

JOE:

Who were the others?

MARY:

Must you ask these questions, Mr. McAllister?

JOE:

What are ya hiding?

MARY:

Nothing, Mr. McAllister. I just find it painful to talk about it. (*slight pause*) My husband, his sisters and their husbands.

JOE:

He had two sisters?

MARY:
Yes.

JOE:
Well—that's six people total. Not five.

MARY:
I wasn't including myself.

JOE:
Oh. (*pause*) Was that his whole family?

MARY:
Yes.

JOE:
All of them just wiped out. His entire lineage ended there. That's a ripe tragedy.

MARY:
I guess it depends on the lineage.

JOE:
Come again.

> *MARY says nothing.*

JOE:
It doesn't sound like you were too fond of your husband.

MARY:
He was a man much like yourself, Mr. McAllister.

> *JOE turns and looks at MARY. He tries to work out whether he has been insulted.*

Scene 6

Lake LaBarge. The boat is tied to the shore. JACK and MARY set up the tent. JACK finds a spot between two trees. He works out where to place the stove.

MARY sings "Do You Remember Sweet Alice, Ben Bolt?" or "Bird in a Gilded Cage" to herself as she finds a spruce bough and sweeps the area for the tent.

JACK puts one gold pan tin on the ground, another on top. He puts the stove on top of the pan.

JACK:
(*looks up at MARY*) It's nice to hear you singing.

MARY:
I feel I've known you all my life.

JACK:
Like family?

MARY:
Yes. Like a brother.

JACK:
A brother?

MARY:
Well—maybe not a brother, exactly.

JACK:
(*hands MARY the tent canvas*) Okay, let's set this up. Throw it over me.

MARY throws the canvas over JACK.

JACK:
(*gropes around playfully*) Where are ya, Mary? Can't find you. (*grabs MARY's foot*)

MARY laughs and dances away. A stovepipe (three
telescoped sections of a pipe) comes through the hole in
the tent. JACK tries to see MARY through the pipe.

JACK:

Can't hide, Mary. I see you!

MARY:

Ssh—don't call me Mary. He might hear us.

JACK:

Mary Mary Mary! (grabs both of her feet)

MARY giggles.

JACK:

Come 'ere!

MARY:

(*giggling*) No.

JACK:

Then, I'll have to come and … (*flings the canvas up*
and bursts out) GETCHA! (*grabs MARY*)

MARY playfully struggles to get away, sees that JACK is
staring at her. She stops. They look at each other, then
kiss passionately. JACK and MARY slide down. Still
kissing MARY, JACK covers them up with the canvas.

MARY:

(*between kisses*) No—we better stop—

JACK:

(*between kisses*) You're right—we'll stop—

MARY:

Your brother—

JOE arrives with an armful of spruce boughs. He stares
at the stove and the writhing bodies under the canvas.
MARY flings herself out from under the tent, sees JOE.

MARY:

I—ah—we—were just setting up the tent.

JOE:

I bet you were. Got yourself a merry widow there, Jackie. (*drops spruce boughs in a pile*)

JACK:

(*emerging from tent, fastening one end to the tree*) We were just fooling around, Joe. Gotta have some fun.

JOE:

Can I have some fun, too? (*smacks MARY on the bum*)

MARY:

(*whirls around*) Stop that!

JOE:

Just having a bit of fun. (*grabs MARY and tries to kiss her*)

MARY:

(*struggles*) Stop it! Stop it!

JACK pulls JOE off MARY.

JACK:

Cut it out, Joe!

JOE:

She's a whore, Jack. Can't you see that?

JACK:

Don't you call her that. You hear me! Cut it out!

The men fight. MARY runs off into the woods.

JOE:

What'd I come in on? What was that if it weren't whoring!

JACK:

That was me, Joe. It was my—oh Christ! she's run off! (*runs into the woods, calling*) MARY! MARY!

JOE:

> (*disgusted, mutters*) Goddamn Hoodoo Whore. (*picks up an axe and chops the spruce boughs*)

Scene 7

> *The woods. MARY is sobbing. JACK rushes in.*

JACK:

> Mary!

> *MARY sees him, starts to run off.*

> *JACK grabs her.*

MARY:

> (*struggles*) No! Let go of me!

JACK:

> Mary, I'm sorry. Joe won't bother you anymore. I'll make sure of it.

MARY:

> How? How will you do that, Jack?

JACK:

> I'll protect you. I promise.

MARY:

> I'm afraid. You can't ever leave me alone with him.

JACK:

> All right. I promise.

MARY:

> And you can't ever touch me.

JACK:

> In his presence.

MARY:

No. Any time. Cause you forget and you get relaxed.
From now on, you be formal with me. I'm Mrs.
Standish and you're Mr. Malone.

JACK:

Seems silly to be so formal in such close quarters,
Mary.

MARY:

Mrs Sta—

JACK:

Please, do we have to start this formal stuff right now?
Soon as we get back to the tent? Okay? (*moves closer to
her*) I'm crazy about you, Mary.

MARY:

Well—(*hesitates*) all right. See, we can't joke and laugh
around your brother. That's what sets him off. There's
people like him and they can't stand to see other folks
happy. They got this little spirit of envy that they carry
around with them and it's like this thing they're
carrying, grows and takes on a life of its own.

JACK:

Let's not talk about him. (*moves in and caresses her*)

MARY:

(*protests*) No—Jack—

JACK:

(*still caressing her*) We'll be formal later. Kiss me now.
(*kisses her*)

> *They embrace passionately. MARY pulls away.*

MARY:

We mustn't.

JACK:

Why not?

MARY:
Well—

JACK:
Can't think of a reason, can you?

MARY:
I'm so confused. There are no rules here, are there?

JACK:
What do you mean?

MARY:
It's like feelings have taken over the rules. I laugh. I cry. I don't know where I am from one moment to the next. One minute, I'm with this dirty brute. The next minute, I'm with you.

JACK:
What dirty—who was this?

MARY:
Oh—oh—just this man—my husband and I met on the Trail—Oh Jack, I'm so afraid! Ever since I got here, it's all been a waking dream to me. Things appear and disappear and if I see something good and I don't reach out and grab it and hold it close, it'll go away.

JACK:
Hold me, Mary. I want you. I want you near me. All the time.

MARY:
Oh Jack.

> *He embraces her passionately. She responds. After a while, JACK takes off his coat and lays it down on the ground as a blanket. He draws MARY down to him.*

MARY:
Do you love me, Jack?

JACK:

You have the most beautiful eyes, Mary. I've never seen eyes like yours before.

They embrace. Lights down.

Scene 8

Lights up. JACK and MARY sit up and adjust their clothes. MARY clings onto JACK.

MARY:

(*playfully*) Brrr! It's cold! (*rubs herself against him*)

JACK shrugs her off.

MARY:

Jack?

JACK:

Yeah.

MARY:

Jack, what's wrong?

JACK:

We can't let on what's happened.

MARY:

Why not?

JACK is silent.

MARY goes to touch JACK. He brushes her off.

JACK:

Make yourself decent.

MARY:

I am decent.

JACK:

    Maybe.

MARY:

    Pardon?

JACK:

    My brother may have been right about you.

MARY:

    What do you mean?

JACK:

    You know.

        MARY looks perplexed.

JACK:

    (*shrugs*) Maybe, you are a whore.

MARY:

    (*slaps him*) (*sobs*) How—could—

JACK:

    Sorry.

MARY:

    I love you, Jack. I wouldn't have done it if I didn't love you.

JACK:

    Stop that.

MARY:

    Don't you love me?

JACK:

    Let's go. (*takes her hand*)

MARY:

    (*pulls her hand away*) Don't you love me?

JACK:

> I don't know. I thought I did. Now, I'm not so sure. (*pause*) You shouldn't always give a man what he wants. (*grabs her hand*) Come on.

MARY:

> You made a promise to protect me.

JACK:

> I know. I told you I'd do it. I'll do it. I keep my promises.

MARY:

> What about the ones that aren't spoken?

JACK:

> They don't count.

Scene 9

Inside the tent. JOE is worried, waiting. JACK enters.

JOE:

> (*leaps up*) Jesus! Am I glad to see you. What kept you so long?

JACK:

> It took some persuasion—(*leads MARY in*)

JOE:

> Aw Cripes, you brought her back.

JACK:

> Well, she can't stay outside all night. You get your nose twisted out of joint just cause we were joking around?

JOE:

> A private joke.

JACK:

Well, it's off. See. It's over. Okay?

At "over," MARY quickly looks at JACK.

JACK:

Neither of us lays a hand on her. That's the deal, eh.

JOE:

Don't know what we need to deal about. She's got no choice. We can do what we like with her.

JACK:

What's happened to you?

JOE:

Whaddya mean?

JACK:

You're like some kind of animal.

JOE:

You're telling me I gotta deal. I'm telling you I don't. Now, if you ask instead of tell. If you say— "Joe, would you please be nice to Mrs. Standish. Pretend to respect the little whore. Would you please do that for me," then okay. Yeah, I'll do it. But let's get this much straight. I'm doing it cause I respect you. Not her. Got it?

JACK:

Okay.

JOE:

And it's me that's making the deal, not you.

JACK:

Okay.

JOE:

Fine, then, we're agreed. Here's some grub. (*hands a plate to JACK*)

After a few minutes, he hands a plate to MARY.

MARY:
(*hands it back*) No dinner for me, thank you, Mr. McAllister. (*curls up in a little ball on her bed, faces away from the two men*)

JOE:
What's eatin' her?

JACK shrugs.

Scene 10

The next morning. Mary has made breakfast. Joe goes out to relieve himself.

JACK:
Great breakfast!

MARY says nothing.

JACK:
How'd you sleep?

MARY does not answer.

JACK:
Why aren't you talking to me?

MARY:
I have nothing to say to you, Mr. Malone.

JACK:
I kept my promise.

MARY:
Please continue to keep it, Mr. Malone. That's all I ask of you.

JOE enters. MARY leaves.

JACK:

How long you figure till we reach Dawson?

JOE:

I dunno. Just pray we get there before the whole
shooting match freezes over. Those little slabs of ice
are starting to team up. (*slight pause*) You and the
Hoodoo were out for a long time. That must have
been some act of persuasion you committed.

JACK:

Drop it, Joe.

JOE:

Am I right?

JACK:

Drop it!

> *Pause. JACK sniffs the air.*

JACK:

There's a funny smell in here. Keep catching whiffs of it.

JOE:

Well, we all stink, Jacky Boy.

JACK:

No—this is—ah—

JOE:

Shite! Forget to tell ya. Bought some fish! (*roots around
and waves them*)

JACK:

Oooh. That's the smell all right.

JOE:

It's dried. It's Injun fish. Two of them paddled up to
the camp last night, while you was entertaining the
widow.

JACK:

I told you—

JOE:

They leap out of their boat and wave their fish at me. I
thought—fish would be a nice change for supper.
Soon as I'm close, I see it's dry and oily and it smells
funny, but it's too late now. One fellah's shoving the
fish in my face with one hand and tuggin' on my
pocket with the other. I'm like—okay, okay, I get the
point!

JACK laughs.

JOE:

It was pretty funny. (*laughs*) They did it like this.
(*waves the fish in JACK's face and grabs his pocket*)

JACK:

Ooh! God! Get it away! (*laughs*)

*JOE pursues JACK. He laughs as he dodges him. MARY
enters the tent as the two men are laughing. They laugh
and carry on with their conversation as if she weren't
there.*

JOE:

(*puts fish away*) So, we got fish for dinner tonight. I
asked them about the river and if I got it right—we
got another set of rapids to get through.

JACK:

Bad as White Horse?

JOE:

Maybe. Not sure.

JACK:

Will we portage?

JOE:

No. We'll run 'em.

MARY stiffens.

Scene 11

That night. Inside the tent. Spruce boughs cover the ground of the tent. MARY shivers and huddles near the stove.

JACK:
> Cold?

MARY nods.

JACK:
> I tried to clear the snow. It's easier to cover it. (*pause*) Do you want one of my sweaters?

MARY:
> No, thank you, Mr. Malone.

JACK:
> Aw—come on, Mary. (*takes her hand*)

MARY yanks it away.

JACK:
> Mrs. Standish, I hate to see you shivering. (*puts sweater over her shoulders*)

MARY shrugs it off.

JACK puts it on again.

JOE enters, clapping his hands to keep warm.

JOE:
> Dinner ready, yet?

JACK shrugs.

MARY dishes food onto plates. She has kept the sweater on. She sits away from the men in a corner.

JACK:

>(*takes a bite*) It's delicious. We're really getting spoiled here, Joe. Thank you, Mrs. Standish.

>*MARY says nothing.*

JOE:

>Injun fellahs told me to keep right and watch for the whirlpool.

JACK:

>That was a humdinger.

JOE:

>Yep. Thought we were goners.

JACK:

>Did you?

JOE:

>Yep.

JACK:

>Geez—you sure hid it.

JOE:

>Didn't want you to panic.

>*Pause. They eat.*

JACK:

>So, Mary's not a Hoodoo, after all.

>*JOE looks up, startled.*

MARY:

>A what?

JACK:

>A Hoodoo. Joe thought you were bad luck.

MARY:

>Oh.

JOE:

    (*to JACK*) You talk too much.

JACK:

    It's a silly superstition, Joe. And the proof's been borne out.

        Sound of a MALE VOICE (HANK) outside tent.

HANK:

    (*off*) Helloo! You in there!

JACK:

    (*starts to go out*) Yeah?

        A man (HANK) pushes past JACK and enters the tent.
        JOE moves to get his rifle.

HANK:

    Sorry to intrude but it's colder than a witch's tit out there. (*sees MARY*) Oh, pardon, Ma'am. I'm Hank Halliday and this is my partner, Pete Smith.

        Another man (PETE) pushes past a bewildered JACK.

HANK:

    We smelled your grub and wondered if you had any to spare. Do unto others as you would be done by, eh.

JOE:

    (*perplexed*) Huh?

JACK:

    Some coffee?

HANK:

    Coffee would be good. Food would be better.

JACK:

    Well, we have some supper left. Not much, but you're welcome to it. (*serves them*) Sit down. I'm Jack Malone. This is my brother, Joe.

JOE nods puts rifle down, but keeps it close by.

JACK:

And … my wife, Mary.

JOE and MARY look up, surprised.

HANK:

Pleased to meet you, Mrs. Malone. (*starts eating*)

PETE nods as HANK speaks, eats.

They gobble the food.

HANK:

(*moans*) Oooh. That's good.

PETE:

Yeah—real good.

HANK:

We'll pay you.

JACK:

That's okay.

PETE:

S'good, cause we don't have nothing, anyways. (*laughs*)

HANK:

(*to PETE*) It's not a laughing matter, Dodobrains.

PETE:

I said I was sorry.

HANK:

He doesn't get it. Our food got dumped in the Rink today.

PETE:

Not all of it.

HANK:

Most of it. And he was supposed to tie it down.

PETE:

    I thought I did!

HANK:

    Well, ya didn't, did ya. This here's a life 'n death
    situation and booby here forgets to tie the food down.

PETE:

    I didn't know there were gonna be more rapids.

HANK:

    That's right. And you know why that is?

PETE:

    No.

HANK:

    Cuz ya lost the map!!

PETE:

    Sorry.

HANK:

    (*to JACK and JOE*) Anyways, we was wondering if we
    could buy some food from you.

JOE:

    I thought you said you didn't have any money.

HANK:

    An I.O.U. Till we get to Dawson.

JACK:

    Sure. We'll give you some.

JOE:

    We're already one outfit short. Three of us, eating on
    two.

HANK:

    (*to JACK*) Crikey! You didn't provide for your wife.
    What sort of husband are ya? Oh hey, I'm just kidding.
    I didn't mean no offence.

JACK:

Joe here lost his outfit in the Squaw.

JOE:

(*splutters*) What!

HANK:

(to Joe) Hard luck, fellah.

JOE:

I did NOT lose my goddamn—

HANK:

Yup. Squaw's dangerous. That party that got drowned. That was awful. Bunch of showgirls brought up specially.

JACK and JOE turn and look at MARY.

JOE:

Showgirls?

PETE:

Macque and his whores, more like.

JOE:

(*triumphantly*) You don't say?

HANK:

Well Mrs. Malone, you make an excellent supper. Thank you. Pete 'n I will be on our way. We just needed something warm in our bellies. And hey, don't worry about us starving to death. There's plenty of berries about.

PETE:

Berries is gone, Hank.

HANK:

Well, we'll—um—find something.

PETE:

>We ain't gonna find nothing, Hank. We're gonna starve.

HANK:

>Don't mind Pete here. He's a worrywart. Time was a fellah 'd give you the shirt off his back. (*to PETE*) But those times is gone, Pete.

JOE:

>Okay! okay! cut the sobsister act. You can have some of our grub.

>*JACK goes to give some to them. JOE stops him.*

JOE:

>I'll do it. You'd be giving it all away. There's enough for two days. Fort Selkirk's up ahead. They'll have something for ya.

HANK:

>Thanks, we're much obliged. And good luck to ya.

>*HANK and PETE leave.*

JOE:

>Macque and his whores, eh?

MARY:

>Showgirls. I met them in Bennett. They were like family to me. Flora, Lily ... (*starts to sob*)

JOE:

>Aw! Not again! You ever notice, Jack, that when you ask her a straight question, she starts blubbering?

MARY:

>(*sobbing*) I suppose you think it's funny having all your friends and family die!

JACK:

>Your family was on that scow?

MARY:

Well—no.

JOE:

See!

MARY:

They died in Seattle. Influenza. It took my mother and brother. I was all alone. I had friends but I didn't want to be their charity case so I came up here.

JOE:

Yeah and HOW exactly did you come up here? That's what I'd like to know.

MARY:

(*evasively*) I had some money.

JOE:

You said your father left you destitute. And after paying for all those funerals—

MARY:

Look, what does it matter how I got here!

JOE:

Pimp and his whores, I'm telling ya, Jacky.

MARY:

You've been wanting to make me into a whore ever since you met me!

JOE:

If it walks like a duck and it quacks like a duck ...

    MARY starts to cry.

JOE:

(*throws his hands up*) JESUS! NOT AGAIN!

JACK:

(*goes to MARY*) Please, Mary. Tell me.

MARY:

A prospector wanted a woman to go with him to the Klondike ...

JOE:

How'd ya meet this prospector? You being such a lady and all.

MARY:

The advertisement was nicely worded—

JOE:

ADVERTISEMENT?!

JOE bursts into fits of laughter. MARY ignores him and talks to JACK.

MARY:

Respectful. I had romantic notions, I guess. About prospectors. I thought Mr. Standish would be a gentleman.

JOE:

Gentleman?! (*howls*)

MARY:

But he didn't write the ad. Some other man did that. Mr. Standish couldn't read or write.

JOE:

And "Mister" Standish turned out to be a pimp?

MARY:

No! He was a prospector!

JACK:

Why didn't you head back?

MARY:

I hadn't a penny to my name. He paid for my passage and I owed him. He was old. He wasn't going to bother me. He wanted to get at the gold and he needed a human pack horse to help him do it. Long as I carried my weight, cooked the supper and held my tongue, he left me alone. (*to JOE*) Sound familiar?

JOE:

See! She's been lying all along! All those tears. All that poor widow crap! I bet you did the deed with Standish. Hold your nose, close your eyes, it's not so bad. Whore!

MARY:

Maybe you should just rape me and get it over with!

JOE:

(*rises*) Maybe I will!

MARY:

Sure. Then, we'll all know what sort of man you really are. Low-life scum! You pretend to be above me. Call me a whore—but what are you? Eh? What are you?

JOE:

Damn you! (*grabs MARY and shakes her*)

MARY:

Go ahead! Do it! I dare you!

JOE tries to pin MARY down. MARY kicks, punches and flails at JOE.

JACK:

(*hauls JOE off MARY*) Stop this! Christ! Are you crazy?!

JACK shoves JOE over to his bed on the other side of the tent. He stands in between JOE and MARY as they sit and glare at each other.

Lights down.

Scene 12

Middle of the night. JACK goes to MARY's bed, approaches it. As soon as he bends down, she pulls out a knife.

MARY:

(*hisses*) I'll use it!

JACK:

(*takes knife away easily*) What the hell are you playing at? (*hauls her out of bed, throws blanket on her*) Come!

MARY:

What—

JACK:

Ssh—(*takes her outside*)

Scene 13

Outside the tent. By the river.

JACK:

I can't protect you, anymore.

MARY:

You mean you won't.

JACK:

You can't shoot your mouth off at Joe and expect me to save you.

MARY:

I'm sorry. I don't know what got into me.

JACK:

> You got his blood up and I don't think I can get it back down again. (*pause*) You better find yourself another situation.

MARY:

> You're just going to leave me here?

JACK:

> 'Course not. We'll find some decent folk who'll take you in.

MARY:

> You mean like Hank and Pete?

JACK:

> Oh no! Not those fellahs. I don't want to send you away but I don't know what else to do.

MARY:

> (*shivers*) Weather turns in an instant.

> *JACK says nothing.*

MARY:

> Do you think it'll turn back? Be nice the way it was on Lake Labarge? (*moves in to JACK*)

JACK:

> (*moves away*) No. Winter's setting in. (*slight pause*) Why'd you lie to me?

MARY:

> I never lied.

JACK:

> You said you were married.

MARY:

> I knew your brother wouldn't respect me unless I said I was—I was frightened.

> *JACK thinks it over.*

JACK:

Here's my deal. You don't say one word more. Not a word. Keep your trap shut and make yourself invisible. And maybe Joe will leave you alone ... Agreed?

MARY nods.

JACK starts to head back to the tent.

MARY:

Jack?

JACK:

Yeah?

MARY:

Tonight ... when those men came in ...

JACK:

Yeah.

MARY:

I thought it was really sweet of you to say you were my husband.

JACK turns to head back.

MARY:

Jack?

JACK:

What?

MARY:

Do you think I'm one of those Hoodoos?

JACK does not answer.

MARY:

That I kill everything I touch? (*moves closer to him*)

JACK:

'Course not, Mary.

MARY:

> Prove it. Warm me up. Just a little. Show me that winter hasn't set in quite yet.

> > *JACK hesitates, then takes MARY in his arms. He kisses her. They kiss for a while.*

> > *The Northern Lights appear as a green misty curtain that threatens to envelope them.*

JACK:

> (*looks up and pulls away*) Whoah! Is that your spell on me?

MARY:

> What? (*looks up*) It's like a curtain.

JACK:

> It's dripping down on us. Do you think I can touch it? (*puts his hand up*)

MARY:

> Don't, Jack! It might—

JACK:

> What? Bite? I'm not afraid of the Hoodoo Mist.

> > *The green mist recedes.*

MARY:

> It's going away. Didn't like what you said.

JACK:

> It's weird. Like someone painting the sky.

MARY:

> Do you think it's been dripping down all these vapours on us and that's why we've all been … acting crazy.

JACK:

> Well, Joe's always been mean. And he is getting worse. But, I don't think it's the sky that's doing it.

MARY:

I've not been myself—since I got here. I've been …
ah—well—impulsive. I'm not usually like that. And—
ah—that night on Lake LaBarge. I don't know why I
allowed that to happen. It's like I've only got so much
time and I've got to make the most of it. I keep feeling
that I could be dead tomorrow. We almost got killed
today, didn't we?

JACK:

(*takes her in his arms again*) There now, Mary. It'll be all
right.

MARY:

(*looks up*) Oh look, it's changing colours.

> *The sky goes from green to pink. They look at it.*

JACK:

It's eerie.

MARY:

I hope it's not the thing that's making us crazy. It's so
beautiful.

JACK:

You're not crazy, Mary.

MARY:

I hope not, Jack.

> *They kiss.*

JACK:

And I like it when you're impulsive. (*unbuttons her
blouse and kisses her breast*)

MARY:

We should go back now.

JACK:

> (*kisses her*) I don't want to—(*caresses her*) Oh—Mary,
> you're so soft and so beautiful—

MARY:

> (*breaks away from him*) Goodnight, Mr. Malone. (*runs
> towards tent*)
>
> *JACK stands, looking at her.*

Scene 14

> *The next morning. MARY has made breakfast. She sits
> on her bed and eats her portion. JACK and JOE are by the
> stove. JOE stares at MARY.*

JOE:

Well, Jack, what should we do with the whore?

JACK:

Don't start, Joe. Just ignore her.

JOE:

Ignore her.

JACK:

> She's not gonna talk now, Joe. She cooks and helps
> out and we leave it at that. (*hands JOE a plate of food
> and some coffee*)

JOE:

You had a word with her, did you? Last night? In bed?

JACK:

> 'Course not, Joe. She just knows what's good for her,
> now.

JOE:

So, she's gonna shut up.

JACK:

Yeah.

JOE:

So, I could say anything I like, she won't say a word.

JACK:

Don't do that, Joe.

JOE:

Like, I could say—only a whore would sell herself off to a total stranger. And a dumb whore, too. Cause she didn't get a good deal. Got herself an ugly old man ...

MARY is furious, but contains herself.

JOE:

... Should have held out for a higher bidder. Maybe, that's what she's doing now, Jack. You're young, good-looking. But you got it for free, didn't ya?

MARY looks away.

JOE:

Oh yeah, Jacky told me all about it.

JACK:

Joe! Cut it out!

JOE:

Said you were desperate for it. There's nothing wrong with that. In fact, in your profession, it's a boon.

JACK:

That's enough, Joe!

MARY leaves the tent.

JOE:

She's got your short hairs all tied up and put a little bow on besides.

JACK:

> We're through.

JOE:

> Well, that's good, Jack, 'cause a woman's always gonna give ya trouble.

JACK:

> No, Joe. You and I are through.

JOE:

> What?!

JACK:

> I'm not gonna be your partner, anymore. We'll divide up the stuff. You go your way. Mary and I will go ours.

JOE:

> You're joking.

JACK:

> No. I'm not. I've had enough.

JOE:

> How do ya divide up a boat? Or a tent? Or a stove?

JACK:

> One of us takes the boat. The other takes the tent and the stove.

JOE:

> That's stupid.

JACK:

> I don't care. I'm not putting up with this crap, anymore.

JOE:

> You'd really do that.

JACK:

> I'll start right now. Food's fairly easy to divide.

JOE:

You can't make it on your own.

JACK:

I won't be alone. I'll be with Mary. You'll be alone.

JOE:

This is insane.

JACK:

Then—lay off her. That's all I ask. It's simple.

Long pause as JACK starts separating the food bags.

JOE:

You can't talk to her, either, then.

JACK:

I won't.

JOE:

Not on the sly.

JACK:

I won't.

JOE:

(*sighs*) Okay.

JACK:

(*goes to the tent flap and calls out*) Mrs. Standish!

JOE:

She ain't married.

JACK:

Miss Potter! (*pause*) She's not coming.

JOE:

Aw, too bad.

JACK:

(*calls out again*) Miss Potter, I talked to Joe and he promises he won't say another word to you, till we get

76

to Dawson. I'm not allowed to talk to you, either. I'm sorry it's come to this. (*slight pause*) So, if you're coming with us, you better hurry, cause we'll be leaving soon.

> *They pack up their gear. Lights down slightly to indicate passage of time.*

> *JACK and JOE carry their gear out to the boat. MARY comes out of the woods. She joins them silently, picks up a load and carries it.*

JOE:
(*mutters*) Waits till most of the work is done and THEN she turns up.

JACK:
Joe.

JOE:
Okay.

> *They work in silence. Lights down.*

Scene 15

> *Days later. Dinner. MARY sits and eats in silence. JOE and JACK talk to each other.*

JOE:
That ice is a bugger. Spend more time pushing it away than moving.

JACK:
I hope the oars hold out. They're gonna be pencils by the time the ice is finished with them.

HANK:
(*outside*) Hellooo in there, Jack? Joe? Mrs. Malone?

JOE:

Christ! Not them again!

HANK and PETE enter.

HANK:

Hi, fellahs, (*nods politely at MARY*) Mrs. Malone. How's your week been?

JOE:

Peaceful.

HANK:

Don't worry. We're not gonna hit you up for food.

PETE:

Though we haven't eaten for the last two days.

JACK:

Help yourself.

PETE:

Aw Geez—thanks. (*dishes out some food for himself*)

HANK:

(*helps himself*) Landed at that trading post up river. They only had condensed milk.

PETE hands JACK a can.

JACK:

Oh—you fellahs don't need to—

HANK:

Take it. We feel real bad taking advantage of your hospitality. 'Specially in view of the situation in Dawson.

JOE:

Huh?

HANK:

Oh.

> *HANK and PETE look down at their plates and eat faster.*

JOE:

What situation in Dawson?

PETE:

Um—

HANK:

(*interrupts quickly*) The situation of getting in there. You have to stay as close to the right shore as possible. 'Cause the ice will send you off to the far shore and you won't get in.

JACK:

That's a good tip. Thanks.

PETE:

Guy at the post told us.

JOE:

What else did he tell you?

HANK:

Aah—Don't try to land in Dawson. Land on the beach before you get there. There'll be tents 'n stuff.

JOE:

Uh huh. And that's all we need to know?

HANK:

Yeah. I'd say so. Wouldn't you, Pete?

> *PETE looks guilty.*

JOE:

(*roars at PETE*) OUT WITH IT! COME ON! OUT WITH IT!!

PETE:

Uh—it's—ah—just—a—famine.

JOE:

> FAMINE?!

HANK:

> Pete's overstating it. It's just a little famine. It ain't biblical.

PETE:

> It could get biblical.

HANK:

> Just a slight shortage.

PETE:

> River's too low. Supply boats got stranded on sand dunes outside Circle City. The folks there took all the grub.

JACK:

> There's no food at all?

HANK:

> None to buy. You eat what you bring in.

JOE:

> (*lunges at HANK*) GIVE ME BACK THAT PLATE, YOU BASTARD!! (*tries to wrest plate away*) Trying to fob us off with a lousy can of milk!

> > *HANK clutches onto his plate, still eating. PETE eats quickly as well. JACK tries to haul JOE off HANK.*

JACK:

> Leave it, Joe! Let him finish his meal!

JOE:

> He's robbing us blind!

MARY:

> OH, FOR GOD'S SAKE!

JOE:

> (*in a rage, to MARY*) DID YOU SAY SOMETHING?

MARY claps her hand over her mouth.

HANK:

I'm sorry, buddy. We didn't want to hit you guys up twice but we're so goddamn hungry. Anyway, look on the bright side. You'll be in Dawson tomorrow.

PETE:

Mind you, you won't be staying long.

JOE:

Come again?

PETE:

Oh. Well—ah—they're asking people to leave. (*brightly*) It's a good deal. If you don't have food for the winter, they'll ship you out on the *Bella*—all expenses paid.

JOE:

Ship you out where?

PETE:

Well—ah. Outside. Downriver—um—to St. Michael's.

JOE:

Back out again?

PETE:

Well—ah—yeah.

JOE:

BACK?! (*starting to erupt*) Jesus F. Christ.

PETE:

Well, there's no point in staying ...

HANK frantically motions to PETE to shut up. He stands up, ready to make a quick getaway.

JOE:

JESUS ...

PETE:

>All the land's sta—(*is about to say "staked" but HANK yanks him away*)

JACK:

>All the land's what?

>>*PETE tries to grab the can of milk on his way out. JOE grabs his arm and bellows at him.*

JOE:

>... FUCKIN' CHRIST.

>>*PETE breaks away.*

>>*HANK and PETE run out quickly.*

JOE:

>We haul TWO THOUSAND POUNDS of CRRRRAAAAP up and down that FUCKIN' PASS! ... (*starts to go on a rampage, picking things up and throwing them around*)

>>*MARY and JACK grab furs and blankets and flee the tent.*

JOE:

>... Risk our FUCKIN' NECKS getting down that FUCKIN' CATARACT they call a river. Chop through FUCKIN' ICEBERGS! Freeze my FUCKIN' BALLS OFF on this GODDAMN RIVER and you say—I gotta GO BACK?! GOTTA GO BACK??!! AAAAAAAGH!!! AAAAAAAGH!

>>*After trashing the tent, JOE collapses on his bed and moans and sobs.*

>>*After a while, JACK pokes his head into the tent, sees that JOE has finished his rampage. He and MARY slink back in. JACK adjusts the tent and stove to make sure it's secure.*

>>*He then goes to JOE and strokes his back to comfort him.*

JACK:

(*quietly*) There there, it's okay, Joe. It's gonna be all right. You just rest. You've had a hard day.

Scene 16

Lousetown. A scattering of tents. JACK, JOE and MARY stand gaping. A MAN rushes past.

MAN 1:

Welcome to Lousetown, cheechakos!

JOE:

Hey, thanks! (*to JACK*) What's a cheechoo?

JACK:

Don't know.

JOE:

Gold Gold Gold! It's all there, waitin' for us. Hey Jacky Boy, you 'n me are gonna be rich!

Another MAN approaches.

MAN 2:

Hey Cheechakos, got any grub you wanna sell? Pay a good price. (*holds out a gold nugget*)

JOE:

Hoooooleeeee! Would you look at that. Isn't that the most goddamn beautiful sight you ever seen in your life!

MAN 2:

So, it's a deal? A few pounds of flour for one of these babies.

JOE:

Sure.

JACK:

>Sorry—no.

MAN 2:

>For two of these babies? (*pulls out another*) Five pounds
>for two?

JOE:

>Sure.

JACK:

>No. We know about the food shortage.

MAN 2:

>Can't blame a fellah for trying. (*starts to go, then stops*)
>They'll be feeding you on the boat. Why not sell your
>grub to me.

JOE:

>We're not leaving.

MAN 2:

>What are ya gonna do, then?

JOE:

>Gonna stake a claim and get some gold.

MAN 2:

>(*chuckles*) Oh, that's rich. You're gonna set your tent
>up around here for a while?

JOE:

>Till we get the lay of the land. Yeah.

MAN 2:

>Okay, Cheechako. I'll be back tomorrow.

JACK:

>We're not selling!

MAN 2:

>We'll see. (*walks away*)

JOE:

Oh man, did you see those nuggets? H-o-oooleeeee!

JACK:

I guess we should set up the tent.

JOE:

Yeah. (*turns to MARY*) End of the line sister. The gravy train stops here.

JACK:

We can't send Mary away.

JOE:

Sure as hell can. (*to MARY*) Beat it!

JACK:

But what's she gonna do? She can't get decent work looking like that.

JOE:

She's not gonna be looking for decent work. Anyways, she can take that boat. All expenses paid.

MARY:

(*to JACK*) I'll be fine. Thank you for everything.

JACK:

But how will you manage?

MARY:

You know I can't stay. (*pause*) You could come with me.

JOE:

What?!

JACK:

I don't want to ship out. At least, not until I've had a look around.

MARY:

I'm not going on that boat. I mean—we could—

JACK:

Oh.

JOE:

She's proposing to you, Jacky. I'd be nervous of a
woman who did that. She's got you all lined up—like a
duck in a shootin' gallery.

MARY:

(*to JOE*) You can't stand to see other folks happy.

JOE:

Happy?! / When have you made …

MARY:

(*overlapping at /*) / Sticks in your craw, doesn't it!

JOE:

… anyone happy? Everyone around you suffers and
dies! // We're lucky we made it to Dawson in one
piece. Hoodoo Whore didn't kill us.

MARY:

(*overlapping at //*) // Jack and I could have a life
together—but oh no, you won't let that happen. No.
You have to turn him against me.

JACK:

That's not true, Mary.

MARY:

Oh, but it is, Jack. Your brother's full of envy. (*to JOE*)
You won't rest till you've reduced everyone around
you, down to your level. You're an ignorant brute and
I'm glad to be leaving! Glad to be rid of you!

JACK:

You don't mean that, Mary.

MARY:

Yes, I do! I'm sick of being good. It's a crock! Frank
Standish wasn't a harmless old man.

JOE:

He was your pimp, wasn't he? Did you kill him? Push him out of the scow?

MARY:

He was a brute and I hated him. I hated him the moment I laid eyes on him. And yes, I wanted him dead! (*to JOE*) And you're just like him! I hope you choke!

JOE:

See! This is what she's really like!

JACK:

Mary?

MARY:

(*shrugs*) See Jack, I'm not a good woman, after all.

JACK:

Was he your—?

MARY:

I won't be selling myself short again. You and your brother deserve each other! (*starts to walk away*)

JOE:

Go back to your whoring!

MARY:

(*spins around, to JOE*) You won't find any gold!

JOE:

Don't curse me, woman!

MARY:

You won't be able to see it. You'll be too busy looking sideways at what everyone else has. Watching, wanting. Always wanting!

End of Act One

ACT TWO

Scene 1

Dawson City. October, 1897. Saloon. Sign near the door says, "Special entertainment—Free with coffee and doughnut $1.00." JACK and JOE walk in and read the sign.

JOE:

Special! That's us!

A man comes out of the gloom.

MAN:

It's about to start. (*takes JOE and JACK's money, hands them two doughnuts and coffee and disappears*)

JOE and JACK sit down at a small table. The room is dark except for a small makeshift stage.

JACK:

It's good to sit down. My legs are killing me.

JOE:

Yeah. Me, too.

Lights on a scaffold, stairs and a MAN WEARING AN EXECUTIONER'S HOOD. He leads HANGED MAN onto the stage.

JACK:

Like low down in the heel and up the back?

The HANGED MAN mounts the scaffold, allows his arms to be tied and a noose to be placed around his neck.

JOE:

Yeah.

JACK:

Must be the boots.

The platform is pulled out from under the HANGED
MAN and he drops into space and dangles. He makes
choking sounds. The audience murmurs and gasps. Just
as it appears that the MAN is about to die, the curtains
close.

JOE:

What the—

The MAN who took their money darts past. JOE stops
him.

JOE:

What the hell was that?!

MAN:

Hanging Man.

JACK:

What sorta town is this?!

MAN:

It's just an entertainment.

JOE:

Grim.

JACK:

Why don't the police—

MAN:

He's a willing party. Gets paid a big wad of dough.

JACK:

You mean the same fellah—?

MAN:

Oh no, different fellah.

JACK:

And you put this show on every day?

MAN:

Nah. New place every time.

JACK:

Why would anyone do that?

MAN:

Why not? No food, no jobs. If ya didn't land anything, you'd want to leave town. So, why not do the stunt and get paid.

JOE:

Suppose, they die?

MAN:

True. There's a risk.

JOE:

Did you see that fellah?

MAN:

After the—(*makes strangling sound*)

JOE:

Yeah.

MAN:

No. Can't say as I did.

JOE:

Then, how do you know he's alive?

MAN:

Come again.

JOE:

If they kill him, they don't have to pay him. And nobody's the wiser.

MAN:

(*thinks it over*) Could be. Well, that's what makes the act exciting. Bit of mystery. Anyways, it makes use of Dawson's natural resource.

JOE looks puzzled.

MAN:

Desperate ginks with nothing to live for! (laughs)

JOE looks at JACK.

JOE:

Let's get out of here.

They leave.

Scene 2

M & M Saloon and Dance Hall. Otherwise known as Pete's Place. A WOMAN (DIAMOND-TOOTH GERTIE) stands behind the bar. She has a diamond imbedded in her front tooth.

MARY:

(*enters*) Excuse me, please. I'm looking for the man who runs this establishment.

GERTIE:

(*laughs*) Establishment! That's ripe. Was just put up two weeks ago. It's Pete's Place 'n Pete's out.

MARY:

Will he be back soon?

GERTIE:

You one of his wives?

MARY:

No.

GERTIE:

What do you want?

MARY:

Maximilian Frost sent me.

GERTIE:

Best you leave right now before you make another one of your morbid jokes. (*ushers her out*)

MARY:

No! You don't understand! I was with him!

> *GERTIE is still pushing MARY out the door.*

MARY:

I'm one of his girls!

GERTIE:

They died!

MARY:

(*starts to cry*) Yes! It was awful! We hit the whirlpool. Flora and Max were thrown out. They were just sucked into it. Their screams! Then, I—(*sobs*) ...

GERTIE:

Lily? You're Lily MacFarlane?!

> *MARY nods yes.*

GERTIE:

But they said you were dead!

MARY:

Oh yes, dead! Our scow spun round and round. Then, somehow, it was flung out of the whirlpool and I was

still on it and then—I don't really remember—I fell
out and went under and—this man dragged me out of
the water and ... and I—ah—I was his prisoner. As
soon as we got near Dawson, I escaped ... and came
here.

GERTIE:
Your poor thing. No wonder you look like hell. Who is
this man?

MARY:
I just want to forget—

GERTIE:
He had his way with you?

MARY nods.

GERTIE:
The dirty louse.

MARY starts to cry.

GERTIE:
It's okay, Lily. You're going to be okay, now.

MARY looks up, tries to stop her tears.

GERTIE:
I'm Gertie Lovejoy. (*extends hand*)

MARY:
(*shakes it, gazes at her*) I like your diamond. It sparkles.

GERTIE:
It cost me some, but you gotta have something that
sets you apart. Funny you showing up like this. The
old place burnt down and all our girls quit to take that
free ride Outside. We was in a bad state. Never figured
we'd get back in operation so quickly. You're a gift
from Heaven. What's your speciality?

MARY:

Speciality?

GERTIE:

Yeah. Buck 'n wing? Straddles? Diaphanous veils?

MARY:

Well ... do you remember my sister, Rose?

GERTIE:

Rose.

MARY:

Yes. Max got confused, too.

GERTIE:

Pardon?

MARY:

Rose was my twin. She had the training. I was just starting.

GERTIE:

You can't sing or dance?!

MARY:

(*hastily*) Oh no! I can sing! I just need—some time—to adjust. Fit in. It's just been a bit of an ordeal. So, if I could do something ... simple?

GERTIE:

Well—uh—sure. You could dance with the ginks. That's simple enough. But first things first. How 'bout a nice hot bath and some pretty new clothes. Sound good?

MARY:

Oh thank you! Thank you so much! (*hugs GERTIE*)

GERTIE:

(*is uncomfortable*) Don't get soft on me, girlie. Gratitude's one thing but expressing it's another.

Scene 3

Another saloon in Dawson. JOE and JACK enter. JOE looks at the gold nuggets displayed above the bar. A prospector sits nearby.

JOE:
Look at those nuggets!

BARKEEPER:
Welcome, Cheechakos!

JOE:
Now, what is that? This cheechee thing.

BARKEEPER:
Means newcomer.

PROSPECTOR:
Or sucker. Here to find some gold?

JOE:
Yeah. Where are the goldfields?

PROSPECTOR:
Not far. Fifteen, twenty miles.

JOE:
That's a long way.

PROSPECTOR:
Thought it was just around the corner, did you, Cheechako. Thought you could just reach into the ground and pull it out, eh?

JOE:
(*to JACK*) We'll head over there, tomorrow, and make a claim.

PROSPECTOR:
(*starts laughing*) Make a claim! That's a good one. (*laughs*)

JOE:

What's so funny?

PROSPECTOR:

Everything's been staked for the last year.

JOE:

What?

PROSPECTOR:

All the good creeks are gone. The gold's been found.
Well, they talk about the Mother Lode but them folks
is just plain greedy. What more do they want? And
yeah, sure, you could go venture out on one of those
little pups that ain't been claimed—

JACK:

Where would they be?

PROSPECTOR:

Beyond the goldfields. Fifty, sixty miles. Probably no
gold on them. Prospecting's a skill. You have to know
the lay of the land. It's like this sixth sense, see. The
land talks to you and you listen. It takes years of
listening to—

BARKEEPER:

What about Siwash George?

PROSPECTOR:

Folks say his brother-in-law found it. Which makes
more sense. Cause Skookum Jim was looking. George
was just hanging around, trying to catch salmon.

JACK:

So, if everything's been staked, what should we do?

PROSPECTOR:

Go back home, Cheechako.

BARKEEPER:

Boat leaves in a week.

JOE:

We're not going back!

BARKEEPER:

You might get a good lay, if you're lucky.

JOE:

No women!

BARKEEPER:

No. A lease on the land. You work someone else's claim and you get half of what you take out.

PROSPECTOR:

'Course the good lays are all gone.

BARKEEPER:

Yeah. They're all worked out. The only ones left are the high risks.

JACK:

High risks.

PROSPECTOR:

Well, fifty percent of nuttin' ain't much! (*laughs*)

A very old prospector (PROSPECTOR 2) enters.

PROSPECTOR 1:

Hey, Bert! Ain't seen you in a dog's age.

PROSPECTOR 2:

Hey Roy. (*to BARKEEPER*) Hey Jake. (*hands him his poke, BARKEEPER serves him*)

JACK:

(*to JOE*) Come on. Let's get out of here.

JOE:

(*watches PROSPECTOR 2*) Not yet. We paid for our drinks. Might as well stay and see if we can learn anything.

JOE goes to a table downstage. JACK follows.

JACK:

> Those guys are just teasing us. Getting a certain
> amount of pleasure out of it.

PROSPECTOR 1:

> Where you been, Bert?

PROSPECTOR 2:

> Out 'n about. (*scoffs down a shot, raises glass for another*)

JOE:

> We don't know how to find the gold, but they do.

PROSPECTOR 1:

> Whatcha doing in town?

PROSPECTOR 2:

> Supplies—bits 'n pieces. Needed some flour.

PROSPECTOR 1:

> No flour. Least none that's affordable. Fifty dollars a
> pound.

PROSPECTOR 2:

> You don't say. (*smiles*)

PROSPECTOR 1:

> What're you grinning at?

PROSPECTOR 2:

> Nuttin'

JOE:

> (*to JACK*) Ever been to the Track?

JACK:

> No.

JOE:

> You was deprived of a proper childhood, Jacky Boy.
> The trick at the Track is to hang around the stable

and sniff out the action. Find out what's up, then make the bet.

JACK:
Yeah?

JOE:
So, that old bugger who just walked in. He's found something.

JACK:
Think so?

JOE:
He has to come to town to register his claim. Then he goes back. Right?

JACK:
Yeah.

JOE:
When he does, we follow him.

JACK:
I need to rest up. Not go off on a wild goose chase.

JOE:
Golden goose, Jacky. It'll be worth it.

JACK:
No—let's stay in town. See if there's work here.

JOE:
You're still thinking about her, aren't ya?

JACK:
Do you really think Standish was her pimp?

JOE:
Had to be. That's why she lied about him. 'Cause she was hiding something worse. You keep peeling back the onion, it makes a bigger stink. And the tears start flowing. Onion tears.

JACK:

She could have told me the truth.

JOE:

You didn't want the truth, Jacky. You wanted to believe she was a lady. Hell, you probably would have married her. Would you have been so quick to marry a whore?

JACK:

No.

JOE:

Gotta face facts.

JACK:

Yeah. You're right. She was just playing me.

JOE:

Fish on the line.

Pause. They drink.

JOE:

I'm not a brute, am I, Jack?

JACK:

'Course not, Joe.

JOE:

We was brought up good. And yeah, I've coarsened some but—

JACK:

It was just another lie, Joe. 'nother skin of the onion.

JOE:

We got each other. That's what's important.

Lights down, then come up.

Later. PROSPECTOR 2 is quite drunk.

PROSPECTOR 1:

You've been grinning like a Cheshire cat all night.
Whadja find?

JOE:

(*nudges JACK*) Psst! The horses are talking.

PROSPECTOR 2:

Oh—nothing much. (*opens coat, displays a glittering rock*)

PROSPECTOR 1:

Holy Christ!

PROSPECTOR 2:

(*covers up the nugget*) Sssh—keep your voice down. I've
left Harry minding the store.

PROSPECTOR 1:

Where did you get that? Colour's not Bonanza.

PROSPECTOR 2:

It's a ways away.

PROSPECTOR 1:

Where?

No response from PROSPECTOR 2.

PROSPECTOR 1:

Come on. Tell me. What happened to the Code. Share
and share alike.

PROSPECTOR 2:

Code's a thing of the past. Stampeders changed all
that.

PROSPECTOR 1:

Well, you old bugger!

PROSPECTOR 2:

(*pause*) My partner made me take an oath. Not
allowed to tell.

They drink for a while.

PROSPECTOR 1:
  You could draw a map.

PROSPECTOR 2:
  Come again.

PROSPECTOR 1:
  Then, you wouldn't be tellin', would ya.

PROSPECTOR 2:
  Hmmm. (*pause*) It'll cost ya.

PROSPECTOR 1:
  How much?

PROSPECTOR 2:
  Fifty bucks.

> *JOE walks over to the bar where the PROSPECTORS sit. He takes out fifty dollars and slides it along the bar to the PROSPECTORS. JACK watches, horrified.*

PROSPECTOR 2:
  (*looks at bill, looks up at JOE*) Who the hell are you?

JOE:
  Joe McAllister.

BARKEEPER:
  I'm in, too. (*puts money down*)

> *ANOTHER MAN who had been sitting in the saloon, goes to the bar.*

ANOTHER MAN:
  Me, too!

PROSPECTOR 2:
  (*groans*) Now, the cat's out of the bag. You Stampeders! You're like bloodhounds. Sniffing out traces. Okay—okay—but only you guys. (*draws the map*)

The men cluster around. JACK gets up to see. JOE comes out of the conclave with a map.

JACK:

Fifty bucks! That's practically all our money!

JOE takes JACK out.

Lights down.

Lights up. Later. The two PROSPECTORS and the BARKEEPER are alone.

PROSPECTOR 2:
Bar cleared out in a hurry.

PROSPECTOR 1:
They all went for your claim.

PROSPECTOR 2:
(*chuckles*) It's a good long way.

BARKEEPER:
Quick. Let's divvy it up before they get wise.

PROSPECTOR 1:
To the ginks!

ALL:
The ginks! (*they toast*)

Scene 4

Goldfields outside Dawson. JOE and JACK digging a hole. There is a pile of wood nearby. Some of it has been used to build a fire. A MAN passes them.

PASSING MAN:
Hey Cheechakos! Gold's not on the hill. It's in the creekbed. (*walks past*)

JOE:

> (*shouts after him*) It's a grave, Moron! If one more asshole calls me cheechako—

JACK:

> We've earned the name. We're a couple of dumb suckers.

JOE:

> If I ever find that old sonofabitch, I'll skin him alive! (*drives pick down into earth*) The ground's so friggin' hard.

JACK:

> Have to light another fire to thaw it out again.

JOE:

> It's like chippin' away at rock. This ain't the kind of digging I had in mind, Jacky Boy. We should be digging for gold. Let's get a lay.

JACK:

> The good ones are gone. Those old geezers weren't lying about that.

JOE:

> Man oh man, did you see how much they were raking out of No.4? Up and down the creek, they're hauling it out and we're stuck here.

> *HANK and PETE walk by.*

HANK:

> Good Lord, if it ain't you two! You guys got a bad lay or what! (*laughs*)

JOE:

> Don't start!

PETE:

> Who's it for?

JOE:

I don't know. Some chump.

JACK:

Olaf Jorgenson. (*to JOE*) Show a bit of respect.

JOE:

Why? I didn't know him.

HANK:

I remember that Swede. Bit of a sad sack. What'd he die of?

JOE:

He didn't say.

HANK:

He was working below Discovery, wasn't he, Pete?

PETE:

Yeah.

HANK:

Poor bastard. (*remembers something, reaches in his pocket, fishes out two nuggets, gives one to JACK, one to JOE*) Thanks for the grub, really appreciated it. (*starts to leave*)

JOE:

Whoah! Where'd you get these?

HANK:

Well, don't know how we did it, do you, Pete? Starving hungry, got so far up the creek. Then Pete collapsed on this claim.

PETE:

Number Thirteen.

HANK:

Guy couldn't get anyone to work it. Unlucky, ya know. He gave us a bit of grub. We felt better, so we signed on. Figuring we'd at least get fed every now and then. Started digging and we hit paydirt! Nuggets as big as your fist!

JOE:

They need anyone else?

HANK:

Now, that's a crying shame, ain't it, Pete.

PETE nods.

HANK:

'Cause if you'd been here a coupla days ago, ya might have been able to squeeze in. But it's all filled now.

JOE:

DAMNATION!

HANK and PETE back up nervously.

JOE:

(*to JACK*) I told you we should have gone right away but n-o-o-o, you had to rest up.

JACK:

From YOUR wild goose chase.

HANK:

Well, we'll be seeing you guys.

JOE:

Stop for a sec, eh? Any other lay look good?

HANK:

Nah—they're all sewn up. You know, mebbe you should jump Jorgenson's claim. Heard it was barren, but you never know. (*he leaves with PETE*)

JOE:

(*throws down his shovel*) Let's go!

JACK:

Where?

JOE:

Get that claim, stupid.

JACK:

You'd go after a dead man's claim?

JOE:

It's the only way we're gonna get one.

JACK:

Let's at least finish his grave.

JOE:

No time. Gotta put stakes down before his friends do.

JACK:

Somehow, I don't think poor Olaf had many friends.
They'd be here digging if he did.

JOE:

You're right. Hadn't thought of that. Then, we got a
good chance of gettin' it. Let's go!

JACK:

No.

JOE:

No?

JACK:

No. I got a job and I'm gonna finish it.

JOE:

I'll go, then. Give me your nugget.

JACK:

No.

JOE:

Give me that fuckin' nugget! (*lunges at JACK*)

They struggle. JOE punches JACK in the face and lays him flat. He grabs the nugget out of his pocket.

JACK:

You're out of your mind, do you know that! Gold gold gold! It's all you care about. It's freezin' cold outside. Have you noticed?

JOE:

So, we'll strike it rich and we'll buy ourselves a cabin.

JACK:

If we strike gold. The big If. Meantime, I'm cold and I'm hungry and I feel like shit. I want food and a warm bed. And I want it NOW!

JOE:

You've been bitching about that ever since we got here. Sound like a goddamn woman! (*imitates*) I want a place to live! Tent's not warm enough.

JACK:

Give me back my nugget!

JOE:

I'm doing this for your own good, Jacky. You leave everything to me. We'll come through okay.

JACK:

You take my nugget. I won't be here when you get back.

JOE:

Sure ya will, Jacky. You'll still be diggin' that guy's grave. (*leaves*)

JACK digs his shovel angrily into the ground. It barely penetrates. He throws it down in despair.

Scene 5

*Pete's Place. The bar. A MAN (PETE) tends the bar. Two
MEN stand at the bar. Their backs are to the audience.*

*The dance hall is offstage or off to one side. A MAN
(EDDY) can be heard offstage, in the dancehall, calling
the dances.*

*MARY wears a simple blouse and a long skirt. She
approaches one of the men at the bar.*

MARY:

Um—excuse me, but would you like to dance?

The MAN ducks his head and hurries away.

EDDY:

(*off*) HOW 'BOUT A NICE QUADRILLE, FELLAHS!

*MARY goes to approach the OTHER MAN. He runs off
before she gets to him. MARY walks around the dance
hall and fidgets nervously.*

*GERTIE walks over to MARY. She is dressed very
provocatively in a clinging Victorian gown.*

GERTIE:

Mebbe you didn't understand me correctly. You gotta
try and get these buggers to dance. You're scaring
them away.

MARY:

They won't talk to me.

GERTIE:

'Course they won't talk! You gotta draw them out.

MARY:

I can't get close enough to do that.

GERTIE:

> Make a fuss of them. Tell them they're handsome. Witty. Clever.

MARY:

> They'd know I was lying.

GERTIE:

> That's the knack. We gotta make these smelly ginks believe they're men we'd want. Flirtin' 'n drinkin's where the money is. Dancin' 's just a means of gettin' there.

> > *The music stops in mid-song.*

MARY:

> Why doesn't the band play the whole song?

GERTIE:

> They never do. You'll be grateful for that. (*mutters to herself*) If you ever get to dance.

EDDY:

> (*off*) BELLY UP TO THE BAR, BOYS.

GERTIE:

> I s'pose Eddy could help you find partners …

> > *A small unprepossessing MAN with a long, black, whispy, handlebar moustache walks into the bar and orders a whiskey from PETE. He is dressed in a black Prince Albert coat and top hat.*

GERTIE:

> Hmm. Bill might make a play for you. He's not shy. Good diggin's there. Doesn't drink and he has regular baths. Could do worse.

MARY:

> Why aren't the other girls after him?

GERTIE:

He's stupid as an owl. That can get exasperating, at times. (*pats MARY's hips*) You better get a belt. If Bill takes a shine to you, he'll load you down with nuggets.

> *BILL notices GERTIE, waves to her, then starts to walk over.*

GERTIE:

(*waving and smiling back*) Jesus! Look at him! Where does he think he is! Paris?! Such a moron.

> *BILL takes GERTIE's hand and kisses it.*

GERTIE:

Why Bill! What a pleasant surprise! That's some outfit you got on!

BILL:

Picked it up in San Francisco. (*smiles at MARY*) And who is this delightful young lady?

GERTIE:

Lily MacFarlane, this is Swiftwater Bill. He's one of our Klondike Kings.

BILL:

William P. Gates, at your service. (*takes MARY's hand and kisses it*) Say, aren't you the Lily MacFarlane who drowned? (*suddenly drops her hand and hurries away*)

GERTIE:

(*shouts after him*) She's not dead, stupid! (*to MARY*) Mebbe we'll dispense with your full name.

> *JOE walks in and stands at the bar. He does not see MARY.*

GERTIE:

(*nods towards JOE*) Ask him to dance.

111

MARY:

(*sees JOE*) Him?! Oh God! I can't.

GERTIE:

There's nuttin' to it.

MARY:

No—I'm sorry. I just can't.

GERTIE:

Listen, sister. You're startin' to brown me off. Are you even Lily? Or are you just some stray bitch feeding me a load of crap.

MARY:

He's the man who held me prisoner.

GERTIE:

(*studies JOE*) Well—he ain't so bad-lookin'. He's gonna show up here sooner or later. Might as well get it over with.

MARY:

I could sing, instead. I'm better at performing, than this—ah—

GERTIE:

Socializing?

MARY:

Yes! Yes, I'm really much too shy for this.

GERTIE:

You poor delicate flower. (*puts her hands on MARY's shoulders, then spins her around and shoves her towards the door*) Cash in yer chips and get the hell oudda here!

MARY:

What?

GERTIE:

You're fired.

MARY:

Oh no, no, please!

GERTIE:

You can't do it. It's a knack and you don't have it.
(*walks away*)

MARY:

Please, Gertie. I'll do it. I just don't know how to start.

GERTIE:

It's simple. You flatter him. Ya pick the very thing the
guy lacks and say he has it.

MARY:

And that works?

GERTIE:

Like a charm. So, what do you hate most about him?

MARY:

He's mean. And spiteful.

GERTIE:

Tell him he's kind.

> *MARY looks at her.*

GERTIE:

And generous.

> *MARY looks very doubtful.*

GERTIE:

Quit yer stallin' and get on with it! I got a show to do.

> *A spotlight comes on a small platform near where
> GERTIE and MARY have been standing. GERTIE steps
> into the light and becomes another person—soft, warm
> and sexy.*

GERTIE:

> Hey there, Boys! (*wiggles her body and smiles, showing off her teeth*) Ain't it pretty! Like it's real money in the bank. The family jewels.

>> *GERTIE sings "Such a nice girl, too." (or another suitable song from the period)*

>> *MARY walks over to JOE and sits beside him. Lights down on GERTIE who still sings through the scene between JOE and MARY.*

>> *JOE is taking a long drink of whiskey.*

MARY:

> Hello, Joe.

JOE:

> (*coughs, splutters, almost chokes*) If it ain't the Hoodoo.

MARY:

> (*about to get angry, stops herself*) Why do you call me that, Joe?

JOE:

> 'Cause you're Bad Luck. It walks and it talks. (*turns her around*) Go in someone else's direction.

MARY:

> I'm sorry I cursed you, Joe. I take it all back.

JOE:

> Good. Now, keep moving.

MARY:

> You're too smart to be so superstitious.

JOE:

> I'm no dummy. What do ya want?

MARY:

> I just saw you and thought I'd say hello.

JOE:

Bullshit.

MARY:

Well—actually, I wanted to thank you.

JOE:

More bullshit.

MARY:

You were—ehem—very kind to me. Very—generous.
You took me in, looked after me till I got to Dawson.
You and Jack saved my life.

JOE:

Oh, I get it. You wanna know where Jack is.

MARY:

No. I don't.

JOE:

Liar! Jack hates liars. (*nods to himself*) I had you
pegged.

MARY:

You have insight, Joe.

JOE:

Huh?

MARY:

Jack's just a boy. I see that now.

JOE:

Tired of boys, are ya?

MARY:

I've outgrown them.

JOE:

That a fact.

MARY:

I like a challenge. How are you, Joe?

JOE:

I'm okay. Got me a claim.

MARY:

Oh my! Claims are very hard to come by.

JOE:

Yeah. It's a good one. And oh, hey, might as well show you. (*pulls out a nugget*)

MARY:

Oh, my! It's enormous! (*strokes it*)

JOE:

Oh, well, it's not so big.

MARY:

Oh, but it is! Did that come from your claim?

JOE:

Uh—Yeah. And you said I'd never find gold.

MARY:

Well, I was wrong, wasn't I, Joe? I was wrong about a lot of things. (*looks at him meaningfully*)

EDDY:

(*off*) COME ON, BOYS! YOU CAN ALL WALTZ!

MARY:

Would you like to dance with me, Joe?

JOE:

Uh—(*cautiously*) Okay. 'Spose I should celebrate my claim.

> *JOE gets up and follows MARY to the outskirts of the dance floor. GERTIE has stopped singing and watches them. The band plays a waltz.*

MARY waltzes with JOE. JOE is a very good dancer.

MARY:

(*surprised*) You can dance.

JOE:

I can do a lot of things you don't know about.

EDDY:

(*off*) LET'S HAVE A NICE LONG JUICY WALTZ!

JOE:

Juicy, eh. Where do those waltzes happen? Upstairs?
(*holds MARY closer*)

MARY:

Um—When did you learn to dance?

JOE:

When I was a boy. Ain't done it for years. But I guess it
comes back ... when you're least expecting it. (*slight
pause*) Never thought I'd see you again. (*pause*) I was
hard on you. It's Jack. He brings it out in me.

MARY:

How?

JOE:

He keeps doing stuff. We was supposed to be alone—
him and me on the Trail. Then, he brings you into it.
I don't like surprises.

The music stops in mid-waltz.

EDDY:

(*off*) PROMENADE TO THE BAR. TREAT YOURSELF AND
THE LITTLE LADY TO REFRESHMENTS!

GERTIE:

(*interrupts*) Nice work, Lily. Did ya get his chip?

JOE:

(*confused*) Lily?

MARY:

(*to GERTIE*) It's all right. I'll handle this.

GERTIE:

Oh? So, now you're an expert.

MARY:

(*to JOE*) Let's have a lemonade, Joe. I'm dying of thirst.

She and JOE head for the bar.

GERTIE:

There's a bar in the dance hall. (*points in the other direction*) Go there.

MARY pretends she doesn't hear.

JOE:

(*to PETE*) One lemonade and a whiskey, please. (*to MARY*) Why'd she call you Lily?

MARY:

It's my *nom de plume.* She's my boss.

JOE:

Oh, I get it.

MARY:

Tonight's my first night.

JOE:

Well, let's go upstairs, then. I can afford it. (*smiles*) Lily.

MARY:

Always trying to make a whore of me. Why do you think that is?

JOE:

Only whores are afraid to use their real names. Besides, what else would a woman do here?

MARY:

Dance.

JOE:

Dance?

MARY:

A dollar a dance. First one was on me. (*finishes lemonade*) Thanks for the drink, Joe. (*heads for the dance floor*)

GERTIE goes up to MARY.

GERTIE:

Don't you get high and mighty with me or you're out!

MARY:

I'm sorry, Gertie. I was afraid he'd raise Cain if he found out he had to pay.

GERTIE:

You didn't charge him?!

MARY:

I won't do it again.

GERTIE:

AW, CRAP! You're hopeless! This is how it's done. HEY FRED!

FRED is a shy gawky man. When he hears GERTIE, he freezes in his tracks.

GERTIE:

YEAH, YOU! COME AND DANCE WITH LILY HERE.

FRED turns and looks in a frightened manner.

GERTIE:

Don't be shy, Fred! Lily thinks you're pretty swell. We don't meet many men with flair.

FRED:

Huh?

GERTIE:

Oh yeah, Fred. You got flair.

FRED:

(*worried*) Where?

GERTIE:

Hear you got some beautiful nuggets in your poke.

FRED:

(*cautiously*) Yeah.

GERTIE:

You didn't give them all to Pete for safekeeping, did ya, Fred?

FRED:

No.

GERTIE:

'Cause you're smart.

FRED grins.

GERTIE:

Lily's never seen a nugget. (*whispers*) Show us one of your nuggets, would ya, Fred.

FRED draws one out.

GERTIE:

(*takes it*) It sure is pretty.

EDDY:

(*off*) AND LET'S HAVE A PEPPY LITTLE POLKA!

GERTIE:

(*pushes MARY at FRED*) You two hop to it! I got something to attend to. (*runs off*)

MARY:

Tell me Fred, what's a fine-looking man—

FRED:

She's got my nugget.

MARY:

It's a beauty. you're very clever to have found it. Do you have more?

FRED:

(*looking for GERTIE*) Where'd she go? (*leaves MARY stranded*)

JOE appears and hands MARY a white chip.

MARY:

Oh.

JOE takes MARY into his arms and starts to dance with her.

Scene 6

Pete's Place. 5 A.M. End of MARY's first night.

The girls pull chips out of their skirts. GERTIE lifts up her skirt. Small pouches are tied to her thighs. One pouch holds nuggets. The other pouch holds chips.

GERTIE:

Cash in your chips, ladies!

GERTIE watches as MARY starts to empty the pockets of her skirt. She has piles of chips. MARY lifts up her skirt to pull out chips that have been stuffed in her stocking leg. (she has not bought a pouch yet) GERTIE stares in disbelief at MARY's large pile of chips.

GERTIE:

    I bin sucker-punched.

MARY:

    Pardon?

GERTIE:

    You brought that guy in, didn'tcha?

MARY:

    No. I didn't!

GERTIE:

    You lie to the ginks but you tell me the truth. That understood?

MARY:

    Yes.

GERTIE:

    Okay. Now. Be honest. Is he a friend?

MARY:

    No. I swear. He is not! I hate him. He's always calling me a whore.

GERTIE:

    (*snickers*) He paid enough to hire a bevy of whores and he got nothing for it, but sore feet.

MARY:

    (*laughs*) My feet are sore, too.

GERTIE:

    Gold will sweeten the ache. Work on your songs and you might make it to the boxes. That's where the real money is. Gink buys champagne at forty bucks a pop. You get ten. Same price as forty dances—only all you have to do is sit. And be friendly.

MARY:

    How friendly?

GERTIE:

Some talking, some listening. Mainly, you sit and help them blow their wad. The poor ginks just gotta spend it. They're scared they'll die before they get it out of the ground.

MARY:

I could ruin that guy, couldn't I?

GERTIE:

You could make his life a living hell.

Scene 7

Outside Pete's Place. MARY leaves. JOE comes out of the shadows.

MARY:

(*startled*) Aah!

JOE:

Did you mean what you said tonight?

MARY:

Joe! What are you doing here!

JOE:

I'll walk you home. It's not safe.

MARY:

I'll be fine. Please go. (*looks at Pete's*) They'll think we're in cahoots.

JOE:

Then, come over here so they can't see us. (*takes her hand—draws her into the shadows*)

MARY:

Please, Joe. Leave me be.

JOE:

It was okay for me to hold your hand, before.

MARY:

Well—we were dancing and—

JOE:

So, I can pretend we're dancing. (*pulls her to him*)

MARY:

And it was my job.

JOE:

It was your job, was it? Rubbing up against me like a goddamn cat.

MARY:

You did that! You pressed yourself on me.

JOE:

And you endured, eh. You suffered through it all. Well, suffer this! (*kisses her*)

> *MARY tries to pulls away. JOE won't let her go. He keeps kissing her. After a while, she responds.*

MARY:

(*pulls away*) Where's Jack?

JOE:

(*lets her go*) Jack, Jack. They all want Jack. He's in the goldfields.

> *MARY turns to leave.*

JOE:

Jacky—well he puts a girl ...

> *MARY stops.*

JOE:

... on a pedestal and she's gotta stay there. (*looks MARY in the face*) You're not the type to stay put.

MARY goes to move away.

JOE:

(*holds her*) He's just a boy. You said it yourself. Look at me.

MARY turns her head away.

JOE:

Look at me and tell me there's nothing between us.

MARY:

You're mean and you're selfish and I hate you!

JOE:

Well, if that's hatred, it sure stokes the fire in you. (*pulls her to him and kisses her*)

MARY struggles, then responds.

JOE:

(*releases her*) You go home now, Mary. And have a little dream on me.

He leaves.

Scene 8

The grave. The next day. The wood has been burned. JACK has finished the grave. His BOSS inspects it.

BOSS:

(*looks into the hole*) That the best you could do? We'll have to nail the lid down tight, keep him from crawling out.

JACK:

I hit bedrock. It was too late to find another spot.

BOSS:

(*studies the hole*) Good thing Olaf doesn't have family—
's all I can say.

JACK:

What'd he die of?

BOSS:

Didn't look after himself. Wears himself out getting'
here. By the time he's staked his claim, he's a walking
dead man. Does he rest up? Not him. Works his claim.
Worked himself to death. Now, do ya want the short
answer?

JACK:

Bit late for that.

BOSS:

Scurvy and starvation. Bad food and then, no food.

JACK:

What is scurvy?

BOSS:

Ooh, scurvy's ugly. Starts in the legs.

JACK:

Oh God.

BOSS:

Goin' up from the heel. A slow steady ache. And
you're tired all the time. Blotches is when it gets bad.

JACK:

Blotches?

BOSS:

Starts with blotches. Then, all of ya gets swollen 'n
black 'n putrid. Think ya have it?

JACK:

My legs ache. How do you stop it?

BOSS:

Suck a lemon.

JACK:

I haven't laid eyes on a lemon since I left 'Frisco.

BOSS:

Old-timers don't get it. You should talk to them. Olaf was in a bad state. Somethin' awful. Had to pour him into the coffin—

JACK:

Could you please pay me, now.

BOSS:

Didn't do a very good job. (*pays JACK grudgingly*) There's another fellah 'bout to pop off—

JACK:

No. That's it for me. I'm heading to town.

BOSS:

No jobs there. (*shrugs*)

The BOSS leaves as JOE approaches.

JOE:

Jacky Boy! Christ, I'm beat. I've been on my feet since I left ya.

JACK pushes past him.

JOE:

What's the matter, Jack? Oh Geez, you're still sore.

JACK:

You robbed me, you bastard!

JOE:

I don't know what come over me. But our luck's turning. I can feel it. Let's go to our claim. We're gonna be Klondike Kings, you 'n me, Jacky.

JACK:

Where's my nugget?

JOE:

I—ah—used it to pay for the claim. Not to worry. We'll be hauling tons of nuggets out.

JACK:

In your dreams! I'm going to town. Get a paying job and sleep under a roof for a change. One of those big saloons bound to need someone.

JOE:

Oh no—I—ah—was in one and asking casual-like— just in case our claim don't pay off. And they said there were no jobs to be had. Not in the whole town. That's why all those people left on the *Bella*.

JACK:

Did you see it go?

JOE:

No. Why?

JACK:

Just wondered if Mary signed on.

JOE:

STOP THINKING ABOUT HER!

JACK:

What?

JOE:

Let her go. She's no good.

JACK:

You didn't see her in town, did you?

JOE:

Now how and why would I see her!

JACK:

    I don't know. Just thought—

JOE:

    You think too much. I'm beat. I need to rest up.
    There's a nice little cabin on the claim. Got your roof
    and a place to lay your head.

JACK:

    (*sighs*) Dead man's roof and dead man's bed.

       They go off together.

Scene 9

    Pete's Place. MARY has a new outfit that is less demure
    than her blouse and skirt. She has a belt-girdle around
    her hips. Small gold nuggets dangle from it. MARY
    dances with JOE. SWIFTWATER BILL stands in the
    background and watches.

MARY:

    There's other men who want to dance with me.

JOE:

    They'll have to wait their turn.

MARY:

    Have you told Jack about our dances?

JOE:

    No. Why?

MARY:

    Wondered how he'd take it.

JOE:

    Bet you're still burned that he didn't come after you.

MARY:

Does he know where I am?

JOE:

Typical Jack. He falls in love real easy. But they can never measure up.

MARY:

You haven't told him, have you?

JOE:

He doesn't know what he's looking for. So, he loves 'em and leaves 'em.

MARY:

He's not like that.

JOE:

No? He could have found you if he put his mind to it.

MARY:

Why don't you tell him where I am, then. Or are you afraid?

EDDY:

(*off*) TIME FOR A QUICKSTEP!

JOE holds out a chip. MARY is about to take it.

JOE:

If a fellah knows he's being conned, is it still a con?

MARY:

(*takes the chip*) Yes.

Scene 10

Jorgenson's claim. JOE and JACK at the bottom of a hole. They are not seen but heard.

The hole is about 4 feet by 6 feet and is square. A windlass, made of a spruce log 6 inches thick and 4 and a half feet long, and resting on two posts about 4 feet high, is set over the hole and the dirt is hoisted in a wooden bucket which holds about 8 pans of dirt. The fire is put in at night and in the morning, the smoke has sufficiently cleared to allow a man to go into the hole. A green spruce ladder is inside the hole.

JOE:

There's a little bit of gold there.

JACK:

Oh yeah. A little bit.

JOE:

Beats digging graves.

JACK:

Yeah, now, we're diggin' our own.

JOE:

What's the matter with you? We found a bit.

JACK:

I'm wore out, Joe. I need air. I need light.

JOE:

Stop complaining and help me light this. Yeah, yeah, that's got it. UH-OH! HOLY CHRIST!

Smoke billows out of the hole.

JOE:

GET OUDDA HERE!!

JACK:

YOU GO!

JOE:

JUST GO!

JACK hurls himself onto the ground. JOE follows. They cough and splutter—narrowly escaping asphyxiation.

JACK:

Jesus, that was close. You okay?

JOE:

Yeah. I guess. I been feelin' under the weather, lately. (*drags himself up, looks around*) That Swede was a jackrabbit. All them holes all over the place.

JACK:

In barren land.

JOE:

Now, don't talk like that. We got some gold. Enough for odds 'n ends. (*slight pause*) I should go into town.

JACK:

I'll go. You're not well.

JOE:

No. I'm fine. The walk'll do me good. (*starts to head off*) You watch over things here.

JACK:

Fire's not going anywhere. I'll come with you.

JOE:

No!

JACK:

Why is it you're always going to town?

JOE:

I'm not—

JACK:

You are! You slip out in the middle of the night. I seen you. What's in town?

JOE:

Ah—

JACK:

You got a girl, there. Haven't you?

JOE:

Well—she's not my girl exactly—but she could be.

JACK:

Why are you hiding her? 'Fraid I'll steal her away?

JOE:

They don't always go for you, ya know!

JACK:

I'm just kiddin', Joe. I wanna meet her. I won't take
her. I promise.

JOE:

You won't, eh? (*starts to laugh*)

JACK:

What's so funny?

JOE:

We'll both go into town. There's some things you
should see.

JACK:

I'll get to meet her?

JOE:

Yeah.

Scene 11

*Pete's Place. GERTIE takes MARY to a small area off to
one side of the dance floor and saloon.*

GERTIE:

Lover Boy hasn't been by lately.

MARY:

He's not my lover!

GERTIE:

Sure coulda fooled me. Foolin' him, too, I guess.

MARY:

That's what it's about, isn't it.

GERTIE:

Yeah. Never figured you'd catch on so fast, though.

MARY:

He doesn't seem as bad as he was.

SWIFTWATER BILL approaches MARY and GERTIE.

BILL:

Why, if it isn't Gertie and the Gilded Lily. Charmed.
(*executes a small bow*)

GERTIE:

Yeah, charmed.

BILL:

(*to MARY*) I couldn't help but notice you dancing the
other night. You shine like a diamond amidst all this
roughage.

GERTIE suppresses a derisive snort and leaves.

BILL leads MARY towards the dance floor.

JOE and JACK walk in at the bar entrance of Pete's.

JACK:

This where your girl is?

JOE:

(*looks around, sees MARY and BILL*) Shit. Look who she's
with.

JACK:

> (*looks in the same direction as JOE*) Mary! (*starts to walk over*)

JOE:

> (*stops him*) She's with a high roller. Might as well sit down and watch.

JACK:

> No. I gotta talk to her.

> *JOE hands him some chips.*

JACK:

> What's this for?

JOE:

> It's her job. You have to pay.

JACK:

> Why?

JOE:

> 'Cause there's one of her and a hundred of us.

JACK:

> Where's your girl?

JOE:

> Maybe you should go see Mary, now.

> *BILL hooks a large gold nugget on MARY's girdle-belt.*

BILL:

> Another to add to your collection. (*fondles the nugget on her belt, then traces his finger along her hips*)

MARY:

> (*draws back*) It's beautiful! Thank you, Mr. Gates!

BILL:

>Come now, call me Bill. Perhaps, you'd like to come to my box sometime and see the show from my advantage point.

>>*JACK walks up to them. JOE watches, tries to catch MARY's eye. She doesn't notice him.*

JACK:

>Mary?

MARY:

>(*turns, sees JACK, is surprised and happy to see him*) Jack?! Oh—my—

BILL:

>Sorry, fellah, I've paid for this one.

JACK:

>You've paid?

BILL:

>You'll have to wait your turn.

MARY:

>Um—Bill—could you excuse me, please. Just for a moment. I'll make it up to you.

BILL:

>Now, don't you be two-timing me, Lily, or I take my nugget back.

JACK:

>Lily?

MARY:

>(*to BILL*) He's an old friend.

JACK:

>Yeah. Just a friend.

>>*GERTIE, sensing trouble, arrives.*

GERTIE:

Billee-doux! We haven't had our dance! (*takes him off, gives MARY a pointed look as she leaves*)

MARY:

Jack! I'm so glad you—

JACK:

(*looks at BILL*) Are you his girl?

MARY:

No. Of course not.

JACK:

(*looking around*) Whose girl are you?

MARY:

I'm nobody's girl. It's my job. I dance with the men.

JACK:

(*fondles one of the nuggets*) That a fact?

MARY:

Yes.

JACK:

Enjoy your whoring.

MARY:

(goes to slap him) I AM NOT—!

EDDY:

(*off*) AND LET'S WALTZ THE NIGHT AWAY—A LONG JUICY ONE!

JACK:

(*grabs her hand and raises it as if to dance*) More lies. Put a chip in the slot and crank 'er up. (*gives MARY a chip and holds her tightly*)

MARY:

(*tries to get away*) How dare you!

JACK:

It's your job, isn't it. Oh, smile now, Mary. I just said something amusing. Your boss is watching.

MARY:

Damn you!

JACK:

You never swore when you were with us. Was that an act, too? All sweet and innocent, 'cause that's what you thought I wanted.

MARY:

I prefer your brother's company. At least he knows what he wants.

JACK:

You've been seein' Joe?!

MARY:

Yes. Too bad you never stood up to him. I lost all respect for you, Jack.

JACK:

Who do you respect now, Mary? Men with gold nuggets? I can't afford your respect right now and if I had all the gold in the world, I wouldn't want it! (*walks away from her*)

JOE walks towards MARY.

MARY:

Jack—

EDDY:

(*off*) AND NOW, A SHUFFLE!

MARY starts to go after JACK but SWIFTWATER BILL takes her hand and sweeps her away in a dance. JOE stops in his tracks and watches MARY. JACK walks up to JOE.

JACK:

You lying bastard!

JOE:

Jack—

JACK pushes him away and leaves.

JOE follows.

Scene 12

Outside. JACK walking. JOE hobbles, some distance behind him.

JOE:

(*wheezing*) Wait up, Jacky. I can't keep up. Don't be mad.

JACK ignores him.

JOE:

Aw, come on, Jacky. Say something.

JACK:

You had her. Did you enjoy it?

JOE:

No. We just danced.

JACK:

Just danced.

JOE:

It's true.

JACK:

You knew all along, you bastard! You knew where she was and you didn't tell me!

JOE:

Look, it was unexpected like. I bought the claim and I went in for a drink to celebrate is all. She come up to me, all friendly. You coulda knocked me over with a feather. (*breathing heavily*) Don't walk so fast. I'm not feeling so good.

JACK:

(*stops*) You okay?

JOE:

I dunno. (*recovers his breath*) Anyways, I kept wondering what her game was. Waiting for the other shoe to drop. Thought she was gonna ask about ya—but she didn't.

JACK:

She didn't.

JOE:

Not then. I know they always go for you, Jacky, but it seemed like, this time, she wanted me. I danced a coupla times. Then more. It's like I was possessed. And when I ran out of chips, I waited outside till she came out and I kissed her. And Jacky, if I wanted her, I could have had her. I know it.

JACK:

Why didn't you?

JOE:

Wanted to give her time to come to me. I worked the claim, thinking I could stay away. But I couldn't. I slipped back into town—

JACK:

To get supplies.

JOE:

(*sheepish*) Yeah. I'm sorry, Jack. I waited till she got off work. But she was never alone after that. So I had to pay to see her. (*laughs*) Danced all our money away. And tonight, my heart was fit to burst. Knowing she was gonna tell you the truth. That she loved me. I didn't want to hurt you, Jacky. Thought you had to hear it from her. But when we walked in, she didn't see me at all. All she saw was you. She never cared for me. Never did. (*suddenly stumbles*)

JACK:

Joe? What's the matter!

JOE:

I'm done in, Jack—(*starts to collapse*)

> *JACK catches JOE's arm and places it over his shoulder so he can lean on him. They walk together, JOE using JACK as support.*

Scene 13

> *Cabin. JOE lies in bed. He is delirious. JACK and the DOCTOR stand off to one side.*

JOE:

Is she here? Is she here yet? I can't see her. (*moans to himself*)

DOCTOR:

(*to JACK*) I'm sorry but he's not gonna make it.

JACK:

Scurvy?

DOCTOR:

No. Typhoid.

JACK:

Typhoid?

DOCTOR:

Yeah. There's nothing I can do for him. After he's gone, you best find another place to stay. It's in the air. Lingers.

JACK:

Oh. Thank you, Doc. (*fetches a tin can and pours out some small nuggets into his hand, goes to give them to the doctor*)

DOCTOR:

Keep 'em. It's a long winter. 'Sides, I didn't do nothing.

JACK puts the nuggets in his pocket.

DOCTOR:

Too cold to bury him. Best to wrap him up and put him on the roof till the Spring. (*starts to leave, turns*) Look after yourself. (*leaves*)

JOE:

Just enough to tease. Claim's like a woman. Just enough rope to hang yourself. Is that how the Swede died? Can't stop thinkin' about him. I can feel him in here ... I loved her, Jack. I think I loved her the moment I laid eyes on her. Just wouldn't admit it. Ornery cuss.

JACK:

It's okay, Joe.

JOE:

I was wrong about everything. Wrong about Mary ... She's not coming, is she, Jack?

JACK:

(*goes to JOE*) Sure she is, Joe. She'll be here soon.

JOE:

I was wrong about the gold, I was wrong ...

JACK:

Oh no, Joe. We found the gold. Don't you remember?

JOE:

Just some skim diggin's. And I spent 'em.

JACK:

Oh no, we found more. We got that Big Pan Out.

JOE:

We did?

JACK:

Yeah. Nuggets as big as your fist. Masses of them.
Golden eggs sittin' in a pile at the bottom of our hole.

JOE:

Really?

JACK:

Yeah, Joe.

JOE:

Jack, she's here!

JACK turns to look. There is no one there.

JOE:

Jack, am I like one of those big shots now?

JACK:

Yeah, Joe. You're a Klondike King.

JOE:

(*smiles*) I'm a Klondike King. (*dies*)

Scene 14

*JACK goes outside. The Northern Lights stream down
from the sky in ghostly dripping curtains. JACK raises
his arms to them and cries out in anguish.*

*His cries merge into a song that MARY is singing. It is
the song that she hummed in Act One, when she and
JACK were setting up the camp (either, "Do You
Remember Sweet Alice, Ben Bolt?" or "A Bird in a
Gilded Cage.")*

Scene 15

*Lights up on MARY, wending her way through the
audience, singing her song. She wears a clinging gold
Victorian lace dress. SWIFTWATER BILL and a crowd of
men cheer her on. GERTIE watches to make sure the men
keep their distance and don't mob her.*

Just as MARY finishes her song, JACK storms in.

GERTIE:

Why don't you gild the Lily, boys!

*Whoops and hollers as the men throw gold nuggets at
MARY's feet. She smiles and stoops to collect them.*

JACK:

MARY POTTER!

*MARY cringes when she hears the name, stops and looks
at him briefly, then goes on with her collecting.*

JACK:

MARY POTTER! MARY POTTER! MARY POTTER!

GERTIE:

Why's he callin' you that?

MARY:

He's mad. He thinks I'm his dead sister.

JACK:

I WANT TO TALK TO YOU. NOW.

GERTIE:

> (*to JACK*) Hey Buddy, calm down. You want to talk to Lily. You buy a box. Otherwise, you're out. (*calls*) EDDY! PETE! HELP ME WITH THIS!

JACK:

> Okay. A box. (*pulls out some nuggets*)

MARY:

> And a quart of champagne.

JACK:

> Come again.

MARY:

> Goes with the box. You want to talk to me. You'll pay for the pleasure.

JACK:

> (*hands the rest of the nuggets over to GERTIE*) It's all I've got.

GERTIE:

> (*takes them*) It'll do.

Scene 16

> *The box.*

MARY:

> Don't you ever call me Mary Potter again! See! I'll have you thrown out faster than you can—

JACK:

> Joe's dead.

MARY:

> What.

JACK:

He got a fever. Typhoid. And he's dead.

MARY:

Oh.

JACK:

That's all you can say? You as good as killed him! You teased him and you wore him out.

There is a pause as MARY thinks this over.

MARY:

I wondered how I'd feel when I saw you. But it's gone. Back then, there was edges and clarity. It was piercing. I was scared and I was alive.

JACK:

Mary?

MARY:

No. It's gone. I look at you and you're just a blur. I see a lot of men and they all seem to want me. It's not personal. If I leave out the drunks and the mean ones, there are about twenty nice men that I could choose from. Decent men. Kind men. Men who'd make good husbands. And out of those twenty, ten of them are stinking rich. So, what would you do if you were in my position, Jack? What would you do?

JACK:

What about love?

MARY:

What about it? What chance has love in a place like this? All these choices. All these possibilities. Love gets lost. I loved you, Jack, but you turned me away.

JACK:

I was wrong. Please come back to me. I love you, Mary.

MARY:

So do a lot of other men. You're starting to blend in, Jack.

A MAN comes in with the champagne. He opens it and pours two glasses, hands one to MARY and one to JACK. The MAN leaves. JACK puts his glass down.

MARY:

You paid for it. Might as well drink it.

JACK:

Yeah and what would we drink to?

MARY:

The new century. It's not upon us yet but you can feel it coming. A whole new world. A world where no one is special and a lay's a lay. Let's drink to that, shall we?

JACK:

Christ, what's happened to you?

MARY:

I'm moving with the times. (*takes a sip of champagne, puts the glass down*)

JACK:

(*grabs her, pulls her into a corner, kisses her, then releases her*) Tell me that doesn't mean anything to you!

MARY:

(*dusts herself off*) You've gotten rough, Jack. Not that gentle boy I once loved.

JACK:

Answer the question!

MARY:

Don't ever do that to me again. Nobody touches me unless I say so.

JACK and MARY glare at each other in silence.

JACK:

You make love to Joe?

MARY:

No.

JACK:

Did you love him?

MARY:

He stood out.

JACK:

(*raises glass*) To your new century, Mary. It's not mine. Never will be.

JACK downs his glass of champagne and leaves.

Scene 17

MARY and SWIFTWATER BILL sit at a small table. They are having coffee and doughnuts. There is a small stage area behind them. Other couples are in the saloon/restaurant.

MARY:

Why did you bring me here, Bill?

BILL:

It's a special entertainment. (*pushes a doughnut at her*) Eat up.

MARY looks at the doughnut, does not eat it.

BILL:

So, Lily, when are we gonna have our long juicy waltz?

MARY:

Let's just keep it light, Bill.

BILL:

Light, my Gilded Lily? (*fingers the nuggets on her necklace*) Shall I take a couple of these off, then?

MARY doesn't answer.

BILL:

Worth your weight in gold. Ever hear that phrase?

MARY:

Of course.

BILL:

Wanna make it true? I figure you're 'bout 120 pounds, give or take.

MARY gets up to leave.

BILL:

What'd I say? 'Course I'll marry you. We'll have a big weighing-in ceremony—

MARY:

You think you can buy everything, don't you, Bill?

While MARY speaks, a MAN WEARING AN EXECUTIONER'S HOOD starts setting things up on the stage. He brings out a small set of stairs, scaffold and a rope.

MARY:

Everything has a price in this world. And the world's all gold that can be weighed out and measured ...

The EXECUTIONER leads JACK MALONE onto the stage. A SMALL CROWD forms to watch.

MARY:

Well, the best things in life are free and anyone who thinks otherwise is a gink. And you're a gink, Bill!

JACK:

Mary Potter!

MARY spins around and looks at the set-up in disbelief.

MARY:

Jack?

JACK mounts the stairs.

JACK:

I love you, Mary Potter.

The EXECUTIONER kicks the stairs out from under JACK. He dangles and chokes.

The people watching murmur and gasp but remain in place.

MARY:

JACK!

MARY rushes to save JACK. BILL holds her back.

MARY:

Stop it! Stop it! Take him down! Take him down, for God's sake!!

The stage curtains close on JACK. MARY still tries to get at him but she is held tight by BILL. He shoves her back down in her seat.

BILL:

The coffee and doughnut's on me and the show was free. Best thing in life, didn't ya say.

He pushes the coffee and doughnut towards MARY who is quietly sobbing. MARY takes the coffee, suddenly stands up and throws it in BILL's face.

MARY:

YOU BASTARD!

She tries to run up to the stage. BILL grabs her and throws her down.

BILL:

Thought I was just some poor simple gink, did ya! Two-timing bitch! (*leaves*)

> *MARY staggers over to the stage and pulls the curtains down. The scaffold is gone. Everything is gone.*

MARY:

WHERE IS HE!! What have you done with him!

> *MARY breaks down and sobs. She makes loud wailing sounds.*

> *The table and chairs are removed, as everyone except MARY leaves the stage.*

> *The stage is now bare. MARY is alone. The Northern Lights play in the background.*

MARY:

(*notices the Northern Lights, stops crying*) I keep thinking I see him. Hanging there, crying out on a choking breath—I love you, Mary Potter. And sometimes, when I stand here under the lights and gaze up into the sky, I think I see his spirit calling out to me and I hear my own ghost calling back—"though my friends are kind, it is not like having someone all your own."

Live in the present. That's what people tell me. The past is dead and buried.

> *MARY looks up at the Northern Lights. They fade and go black.*

The End

 Too heavy handed.

The M & M Saloon and Dance Hall—Pete's Place

"Pete's" was a two-story log building, the upper story being the living rooms of the proprietor. One entered from the street, in a whisk of steam that coated the door-jamb with snowy frost, into a low-ceiled room some 30 by 40 feet in dimensions. The bar, a pine counter stained red, with a large mirror and bottles and glasses behind, was on the left hand. A lunch counter stood on the right, while in the rear and fenced off by a low wooden railing, but leaving a way clear to the bar, was the space reserved for dancing. Here, in the glow of three or four dim, smoky kerosene lamps, around a great sheet-iron "ram-down" stove, kept always red-hot, would be found a motley crowd—miners, government officials, mounted policemen in uniform, gamblers, both amateur and professional in "citified" clothes and boiled shirts, old-timers and newcomers, claim-brokers and men with claims to sell, busted men and millionaires—they elbowed each other, talking and laughing, or silently looking on, all in friendly good nature.

Pete himself, one of the few saloon-keepers who had not been miners in the "lower country," served the drinks behind the bar in shirt-sleeves, with his round head and bulldog expression, hair carefully oiled and parted and dark, curled moustache, smiling, courteous and ignorant—a typical "outside" bartender.

The orchestra consisted of a piano, violin and flute and occupied chairs on a raised platform in one corner of the dance floor. The ladies were never backward in importuning partners for the dance; but any reluctance up the part of would-be dancers was overcome by a young man in shirt-sleeves, who in a loud, penetrating voice would begin to exhort: "Come on, boys—you can all waltz—let's have a nice, long, juicy waltz"; and then, when three or four couples had taken the floor, "Fire away!" he would call to the musicians and then the fun began. When the dancers had circled around the room five or six times the music would stop with a jerk, and the couples, with a precision derived from long practice, would swing towards the bar and push their way through the surging mass of interested lookers-on, or "rubber-necks" in fur caps, Mackinaws and *parkas* and line up in front of the bar.

"What'll you have gents—a little whiskey?"

Sacks were tossed out on the bar, Pete pushed in front of each "gent" a small "blower," and the "gent" poured in some gold dust, which Pete took to a large gold-scale at the end of the bar, weight out $1 and returned the balance to the sack. The lady received as her commission on the dance a round, white ivory chip, good for 25 cents ... *

*   Adney, Tappan. *The Klondike Stampede.* 1899. Reprint.Vancouver: UBC Press, 1995, 1997, 2000, 339–340.

Big Pan Out

The men on the creeks lived in a still more sinister scene. It was one of tree stumps and clawed-back earth, of ashes, of heaps of fresh dirt lying in gravelike mounds between shrouds of smoke. An occasional live flame shot out of a pit, lighting the snow, but for the most part the gulches were choked with a cheerless haze and appeared to be, as some imagined, the corridors of hell. The men were underground, scraping, crawling on all fours, mesmerized, straining their eyes for infinitesimal bits of gloss. The quest was noiseless ...

When they couldn't stand the labor and the loneliness any longer the men took the trail for Dawson. In one of the saloons an act that was the talk of the creeks in 1898 was being put on. A man mounted a realistic-looking scaffold, permitted his arms to be tied and a noose placed around his neck. The platform was then pulled from under him and he dropped into space to dangle until his face turned purple. At that point the curtain was drawn. A different man was recruited every night so that the customers could not be sure whether or not the hanged man lived through the ordeal. It added to the horror of it for them to remain in doubt. The show was free. It went along with the price of a drink or of a cup of coffee and a doughnut. "Coffee and" was $1.25, whiskey was 50 cents ...

Popular songs of the day included, "Put Your Arms Around Me, Honey," "After the Ball," "Doris, My Doris," "Two Little Girls in Blue," "The Bird in a Gilded Cage," "Comrades, Comrades" and "Just as the Sun Went Down," as well as the ageless "Genevieve." Many of Stephen Foster's ballads were sung, also. Other tunes heard during the nineties made popular by New York and London shows, were "Ta-Ra-Ra-Boom-De-Ay" "There'll Be a Hot Time in the Old Town Tonight," "You Don't Have to Marry the Girl," "That Up-to-date Girl of Mine," "She Got it Where McDooley Got the Brick," "Put Me Off at Buffalo," "Down Went McGinty," "I'm the Man Who Broke the Bank at Monte Carlo," "I Got Mind," "Across the Bridge He Goes," "The Gold Miner's Dream" and "The Old Stage Door." Many lyrics of the period still survive such as "Only One Girl in the World for Me," "The Sunshine of Paradise Alley" and "Somebody Loves Me."*

• Winslow, Kathryn. *Big Pan Out*. New York: W.W. Norton & Company, 1951.

Klondike Diary

July 17, 1897 "Klondike Kings" arrive in Seattle. Word of the big gold strike hits the newspapers.

By July 27, 1897, 1500 people had left Seattle to seek their fortune in the Klondike.

The characters in Wanted *follow a slightly different time-frame than Robert Medill and his companions. My characters are travelling down the Yukon from Miles Canyon in mid-September.*

Weather Conditions for Robert Medill and Company

Saturday, August 28th—left Seattle on "The Williamette."

Sept 4—arrived in Dyea.

Sept 9–16—cold rain from Dyea to Sheep Camp.

Sept 16th—raining and snowing on the Pass, flood swept away Sheep Camp.

Sept 24—Oct 1st. Crater Lake to Lake Linderman—nice weather no snow, sunny, dry—building boat.

Sept 30—Oct 7th (took 8 days—3 men).

Oct 1st—Froze hard.

Oct 7th—launched boat, used sail, then oars, had small accident on rocks—cost several days time—had to dry and recalk boat—go to head of Lake Bennett.

Oct 15th—Yukon River jammed near Dawson, then broke loose again.

Oct 16th—Medill heading for Miles Canyon—The Squaw—flew past it—out of mouth of Miles Canyon—few hard pulls to shore

Oct 17th—cleared canyon, pack over camp, headed for White Horse Rapids—The Spout camped upper end of Portage.

Oct 18th—let boat empty along wall in eddy below, then portaged stuff halfway to Lake Labarge.

Oct 19th—Lake Labarge.

Oct 20th—left lake, good camps for several days Big Salmon River, ice flow coming out weather turned cold—4" snow, still snowing.*

---

* Summarized from Medill, Robert B. *Klondike Diary: True Account of the Klondike Rush of 1897–1898.* Portland, Oregon: Beattie & Company, 1949.

Setting Up Camp
(In Snow and Ice)

When the weather got colder and ice started to form on the river, the boat was unloaded and outfits were stacked on the bank. The ice froze farther out each day, so it would have to be cut away before the boat could come in to shore.

The tent was hung between two trees. A spot was picked out for the stove. The snow was kicked aside. One gold pan was placed face down on the ground. The other on top and then the stove. Spruce boughs were placed over the rest of the ground on top of the snow, or the snow was brushed away. Bedrolls were used as seats, spruce boughs as beds.

The opened tent was thrown over a person who stood by the stove. The three telescoped joints of pipe were pushed through the pipe hole in the tent. The tent's ridge rope was fastened to the trees.

The stove was always filled with wood before breaking camp.